MOLLIE

WHO?

Tamsen Leigh Emerson

MOLLIE

THE JOURNAL OF
MOLLIE DORSEY SANFORD IN NEBRASKA
AND COLORADO TERRITORIES
1857-1866

With an introduction and notes by
DONALD F. DANKER

UNIVERSITY OF NEBRASKA PRESS · LINCOLN/LONDON

Copyright 1959 by the University of Nebraska Press
First Bison Book printing: 1976

Most recent printing shown by first digit below:

3   4   5   6   7   8   9   10

Manufactured in the United States of America

Library of Congress Cataloging in Publication Data

Sanford, Mollie Dorsey, 1838 or 9–1915.
    Mollie : the journal of Mollie Dorsey Sanford in Nebraska and Colorado Territories, 1857–1866.

    "A Bison book."
    1. Frontier and pioneer life—Nebraska. 2. Frontier and pioneer life—Colorado. 3. Nebraska—History. 4. Colorado—History—To 1876. 5. Sanford, Mollie Dorsey, 1838 or 9–1915. I. Title.
[F666.S36 1976]   978.2'02   75–8764
ISBN 0–8032–5826–7

CONTENTS

Mollie's West

MOLLIE DORSEY's journal was written against a background
of historical events which shaped her destiny and that of her
friends. Nebraska Territory, to which her father, William
Dorsey, brought his wife and eight children in the spring
of 1857, had been open to white settlers less than three
years. Prior to its territorial organization, the Nebraska
region—which some had labeled a part of the Great American Desert—had been Indian Country from which white
settlers were excluded by law. It had been created a
territory on May 30, 1854, by a provision of the Kansas-
Nebraska Act, a measure that was in itself one of the points
of controversy between North and South. To Mollie's
father, however, Nebraska represented an opportunity to
obtain one hundred and sixty acres of land at a lower price
than he could buy it in the settled states. The pre-emption
law of 1841 provided that actual settlers could select land
from the public domain and have the first chance to buy it
at $1.25 per acre when the government offered it for sale.
Land was a powerful attraction to a man with sons.

Nebraska Territory was a huge area of approximately
351,588 square miles, but the settled portion, with few ex-
ceptions, extended only a few miles back from the Missouri
River. The treeless prairie was a strange environment to
pioneers venturing out of the forests of the East and was
avoided so long as land was available along the timbered
streams. Dorsey and other Nebraska settlers of the Fifties
could and did build the log cabins traditional to the Ameri-

can pioneer. The sod-house era of the frontier was to come in later years after the wooded land was settled.

Nebraska provided a highway for westward travel as well as an opportunity to obtain land. The great overland trails followed the natural roadway of the Platte Valley. The freighters and their wagon trains which Mollie Dorsey saw in Nebraska City transported the goods needed for the conquering of other frontiers in Colorado, Utah, and Montana. Freighting was extensive business on the frontier carried on by operators big and small, ranging from farmers hauling their farm produce across the prairie to Fort Kearny, to huge organizations such as Russell, Majors and Waddell with over eight thousand yoke of oxen and fifteen hundred employees operating out of Nebraska City.

The frontier described in Mollie's journal was a fluid and moving area. Men of energy and restless nature often only hesitated in one locality before they moved on to new opportunities. Mollie's journal records such a movement and emphasizes the considerable number of persons who figured in the beginnings of Nebraska Territory and who also were pioneers in Colorado.

Gold rather than land was the goal of the Colorado pioneers. Gold discoveries in the area had been made as early as 1850, but it was not until 1858 that prospectors made the discoveries which touched off the Pikes Peak Gold Rush of 1859. The rather modest findings of the prospectors were reported in exaggerated accounts by newspapers along the Missouri River in Nebraska, Kansas, and Missouri. In 1859 a full-fledged gold rush began, and the trails across Nebraska and Kansas were crowded with gold seekers. In 1860 there was another rush composed of persons described as more orderly and more determined than those of the previous year. Free gold that could be easily found was soon gone, and many disappointed men returned eastward, cursing the newspapermen and Missouri River communities which they felt had misled them for profit. The threats of disgruntled returning Pikes Peakers so frightened the citizens of Omaha, Nebraska, that weapons from the territorial arsenal were issued to citizens for protection. It is estimated that of the one hundred thousand persons who set out for Colorado, twenty-five thousand remained there to mine the gold and lay the foundations of the territory. Denver, founded in 1858, became a boom town where buildings seemed to spring up overnight and prices soared as rapidly.

History moved at a swift pace, and the excitement of the gold rush was still fresh when the Civil War became the overriding consideration. The First Regiment of Colorado Volunteers was raised and helped to stop the thrust of the Confederate General Sibley and his Texans into northern New Mexico. Confederate troops never fought in Colorado, but Indian warriors did. In 1864 the unfortunate Sand Creek Affair aroused the tribes to raids which had outlying settlers fleeing into Denver, and so disrupted traffic on the freighting roads that flour sold for $27 a hundred pounds.

The journal of Mollie Dorsey Sanford was recorded on the Nebraska and Colorado frontiers during years which were of importance and interest in the history of the American West. It is a document of social and historical importance for the student of pioneer life on the Plains, of the Colorado Gold Rush, and of the Civil War as it affected the Colorado frontier.

DONALD F. DANKER

MOLLIE

Denver, Colorado
Feb. 1st, 1895

I have been very ill, and in my convalescence have determined to recopy my old journal, as the original by going through a flood while camping in the mountains is almost obliterated, and only can be deciphered by myself.

I will and bequeath this book after my husband and myself are through with it, to my oldest grandson Bertie Williams. I hope to live to see him grown to young manhood, but life is uncertain. I trust what is worthy of emulation he may profit by.

It is of more value to me than it could possibly be to my children, but I desire that it shall be kept in the family and treasured as a relic of by-gone days, not from any especial merit it possesses, but because I do not want to be forgotten.

While I do not *pose* as a heroine, I know that I have had peculiar trials and experiences, and perchance *something* I have said or done may be a help to my posterity, for trials and tribulations come to all.

May the faith that has sustained *me* through all up to the present be with my children and children's children always.

MOLLIE E. SANFORD

CHAPTER ONE

Indianapolis to Nebraska City

March 23, 1857—May 27, 1857

Indianapolis, March 23, 1857
At Home — Sabbath — P.M.

Before starting for the "far west" upon the journey we have been so long preparing for, I have decided to commence a diary, or daily Journal, to note passing events, to have a confidante or bosom friend, now that I am to leave so many near and dear. I go among strangers, into a strange land, and it may be a long time before I find one to whom I can confide my joys and sorrows.

I have thought for years that I would keep a Journal. I know it is a source of improvement and pleasure, and have only postponed it, because I have thought my life too monotonous to prove interesting. In going to a new country, where new scenes and new associations will come into my life, there *may* be *some* experiences worth recording. At least the employment will divert my mind in many a lonely hour. Everything in life must have a beginning. Let this be the preface to my Journal.

[1]

I have just returned from Sabbath School, the last I shall attend in my old home. Ere another comes, I shall be well out into the wilderness. I regret to leave my class of boys. I have taught them for three years. Dear manly little fellows, I shall carry their bright faces away with me. I am asking myself if, in these years of teaching, have I accomplished any good. Has my example been such as to give them faith in the lessons I have taught?

The day is cold and cheerless, not a ray of sunshine to chase away the sadness of my heart. All of the bright anticipations of the probable interest of our trip does not compensate me for the sorrow at parting from friends.

Mollie Shellenberger and I took our last ramble together today. We have been bosom friends and classmates for years. We vowed *"eternal friendship,"* and wept as only loving friends can weep, to think that we must part—"perhaps forever."

It is hard too, to sever my relations with the North St. Chapel, with whose interests I have been associated since its birth, from the time a mere handful of people held services in my Grandfather's school house, up to the present, with a commodious chapel and regularly appointed minister.

Within its walls I made the start in a Christian life. I hope to find a place for my church letter away out in Nebraska, but O! dear! I don't know if there are any churches there. Some missionary work for you *there*, Mollie, perhaps.

Indianapolis has been my home for years. Here I have had the benefits of schools, churches, and the best of society. I go to a wild unsettled country, where I shall be deprived of all of these; but I go with my dear parents, to share their burdens, and their lot, whatsoe'er it be. I am now eighteen years of age, and must begin to assume life's responsibilities, and not shrink from unpleasant and untried realities. I have had a pleasant girlhood, but have learned even now that we cannot go through life "on flowery beds of ease."

We are a large family. My father and mother have eight children. I am the eldest, and perhaps more relied upon for help and sympathy. My father has met with reverses, and is obliged to make a change. It is very hard in a city like this for one pair of hands to support so large a family. There come alluring inducements to go to Nebraska, where he can take up land. Our two uncles, George and Charles, have urged us to come.

After all, there is something fascinating in the thought of the opening up of a new life, a change so complete as this will be.

We have sold our dear old home. The roof beneath where we have spent so many happy days now shelters strangers, and we are occupying rented rooms until we leave.

We are a happy family. My sister Dora is two years my junior, "Sweet Sixteen," a warm-hearted, impulsive girl, hardly sentimental enough to have formed any serious heart attachments, and is in extacy over the trip. Anna is fourteen, a delicate girl, but keenly alive to anything exciting, bright and witty, generally shielded from the rougher burdens of life, on account of her health. Sam is our oldest brother, a bright manly boy of twelve, a very practical boy, matter-of-fact, everything coming to him as a matter of course. Ada is our darling pet sister, the ministering angel of the household. Will, a merry happy boy of eight, knocks his heels together, and shouts, "Hurrah! for Nebraska!" Dent and Charlie are our baby brothers, too young to understand the change.

I go to church tonight with Court Whitsit. He ranks among my best gentlemen friends. I wonder if he was in earnest this morning when he said "I should not go"? Yes! I know and *have* known there was more than a feeling of friendship on his part, and I am so sorry, for he is so honest

[3]

and sincere. I hope I have not given him too much encouragement. He says I have not. Jen Springer says I am a flirt. I suppose she thinks so, because her "Sweet William" left her side the other evening to talk to me, but there! I've written enough for one time and it is nearly church time. I have no business commenting thusly.

Monday, March 24th

Began packing our household goods. O! dear me, with all the children, and neighbors' children, and constant interruptions from callers, it has been hard work.

Court came last night, but we did not go to church. He was too solemn for anything, and I could "stay and go into a home of my own tomorrow"—if I were ready, and if he were the One. I am glad to go from here "heart whole and fancy free." My experience two years ago, has cured me from falling in love in a hurry. "We loved and we parted," and I hope nothing but good will come to "Jim." I did not know my heart then. Have two years given me much more wisdom? Would it have been wise to have accepted Mr. Horniday's offer? He is a western farmer, and while here on a visit to his brother, proposed. I should not feel flattered, for he came home to hunt a wife, and I suppose I was the first girl that he met.

March 26th

Jennie Springer came for me to spend the night with her. She gave me a package that I was not to open until I got to Nebraska. I suspected something, for she has always been a warm friend of "Jim's." I opened it then and there! and sure enough! there was a picture of him, bright and handsome as ever! I could not take it, of course. I half suspected a meeting had been planned, so came home. It spoiled my last visit there, for altho I have no tender feeling for "Jim," I feel sorry that he does not forget *me* and would not wound him.

Uncle Milton and Aunt Eliza took dinner with us today. Auntie fears we are going to be *heathen* and maps out a doleful future.

Tomorrow we leave, so good-by my Journal dear. When I again greet you, I shall be miles away from the old home, on, on to the new—farewell to the old.

> The tears will come,
> Yes, tears of sorrow fall,
> To think that I must go,
> Must say "good-by" to all.

I wonder who will shed tears of regret for me? Court *looked* the tears *he* could not weep (my good old Court).

St. Louis, Missouri
March 28th

We left Indianapolis last night on the 9 o'clock train, and arrived here at two o'clock today. We were tired and starved, but had to take a cold dinner (I hope we'll have a good supper).

The trip on the cars was very tiresome, and I feel as if I had been shaken up and tumbled out of a four-story window. We crossed the Mississippi River on the steam ferry. We are stopping at the "Missouri Hotel."

March 29th

Mother and I have spent the day in shopping, laying in a stock of clothing. We are all equipped with our spring bonnets. I wonder where we will go to wear them? for the people here say, it is nothing but a wilderness. These reports make Mother look blue, and father a little anxious. Really, we do not know, only that it is a "New Country" and that we are "Emigrants." People say, "Going to 'New

[5]

Brasker'? Nothing to eat there," so, as we do not want to starve, we have laid in a stock of provisions, a whole barrel of sugar, a large cook stove and an elegant set of dishes, so we are all right as long as they last, the sugar and provisions.

Father has our tickets. We go on the boat "Silver Heels," take passage tonight. There seem to be lots of passsengers. I went on board with father. Hope we will have a jolly time.

On board "Silver Heels" *
Sunday, March [30th]

We started from St. Louis at sunset yesterday. I believe there are 500 passengers, lots and "slathers" of young men. We are too crowded to make it real pleasant. The cabin is like a parlor, but the state rooms are suffocating. Could not sleep last night for fear of an accident. This is my first journey upon water and I am a little nervous.

Have been introduced to a large number of people. Our Capt. is grand, and tries to make it pleasant. I have fallen in love (do not expect me to say with a man, Journal dear) but with a darling girl! Libbie Scudder. She is a New England girl, not at all pretty but so attractive I am fascinated with her. She kissed me good-night and said "we would be friends."

We have a motley crew, persons of every form, size, and color. Fussy old ladies with their poodle dogs. Anxious mammas in mortal terror lest their youngsters should fall overboard; giddy young girls, frolicksome children, fascinating young gents, and plenty of bachelors, who fly to

---

* The *Silver Heels* was built in Louisville, Kentucky, for Major Barrows, her chief owner and captain. The ship, named for a fine thoroughbred horse, cost $32,000 and was described as "one of the best specimens of skill and mechanical art that has ever been turned out." It boasted staterooms, saloons, a nursery, and landscapes sketched on the stateroom doors as well as water wheels 29 feet in diameter [*Nebraska News,* Nebraska City, N. T., March 28, 1857].

their state rooms to hide from the females, and romping children.

The immigration to Kansas and Neb. is immense, and we shall see *lots* of people (I guess). We travel very slowly. Our Capt. is careful of his cargo of precious souls.

Friday, April 4th

We are gliding smoothly over the turbid stream. The muddy, muddy Missouri. We stopped at Werton, a small town on the river, today.

Libbie and I must be "affinities" sure enough. She has shown me the picture of her lover, from whom she has been ruthlessly torn. The family actually came West, to get her away from him. She declares she will be true to him for years, and forever.

We were introduced to Dr. Latta * today. Capt. Barrows says he is a great "catch." We have fine music, both vocal and instrumental. There is a creole porter who plays the guitar, and when he sings I almost feel as if I were ascending, so lovely does it sound. He plays for Libbie and I quite often. We have splendid times—flirt all day (or Libbie does, for she calls it flirting, altho it does not seem to me to be just that). I sleep soundly, now, with no fears of disaster.

I sometimes do not believe Libbie is as broken-hearted as she claims to be. She is older than I, by four years. She calls me the young "Innocent." I wonder if I *am* not a little hoosierish, and unsophisticated? I haven't seen as much of the world as she, and I know I've a great deal to learn.

Father and Mother are enjoying themselves. They are fond of singing, and have met some good singers. We are

---

* Dr. William S. Latta became a prominent Nebraskan. He was a member of the territorial legislature, assistant surgeon of the Second Nebraska Cavalry Regiment during the Civil War, and organizer of Cotner Medical College, Lincoln, Nebraska. Among his papers at the Nebraska State Historical Society is a short manuscript poem inscribed "Lines written to Miss Libbie P. Scudder."

almost like one family, such good cheer and such good fellowship, and I never had a nicer time.

I have been real pleasant to Mr. Barlow (widower) because he seemed such a nice old gentleman, and has been so nice to me. The snows of 50 winters have somewhat bleached his scanty locks, but he is as spry as any of the younger men. He is generous with his donations of sweet meats. Today while munching candy, he sat by my side, and began talking sentimental. We had been on deck looking at some elegant household furniture he was shipping. There was a fine carriage, and when I said, "I wish it were mine," he said, "They shall *all* be yours, if you say the word." Would *I* be an old man's darling? Would I? *I* might have wilted then and there, had I not seen his daughter's frowning face, above her baby's curly head, as she called him hurriedly to her side. Her little girl came timidly to my side afterward and said, "My Grandpa lovth's you."

Mrs. Miller saw the tableaux and wants me to fool him, because he is such an old simpleton.

Heigh ho! Mr. Barlow,
I'll think of the matter and let you know.

April 5th

Libbie has coaxed the history of my love scrape, with Jim. Come to find out, she has had a dozen. She has a way of rolling her big grey eyes that perfectly captivates the gentlemen. She writes for several papers and magazines. She has had a peep at my journal. I wonder if she has seen my comments about herself. She knows I love her. She is actually the most interesting girl I have ever met.

Dora has found a pleasant companion in the person of Mr. Armstrong. He likes quiet girls and she is as demure as a kitten.

Mr. Purcell is a nice gentleman, and I enjoy many quiet talks with him.

Mr. Hill is a tall, dark, indolent fellow from Mississippi, a planter. We have some arguments on slavery. Libbie says not to argue *too* much with the fellows, make them think they know it all. That is why she is so popular, I suppose.

Sunday, April 6th

Weather cold and oh! *so* disagreeable. We are making slow progress. There is no promenading the deck today. Quite a number of our passengers have stopped off at different points along the route. We are now in Kansas Ter. The scenery is more attractive. On one side are steep bluffs that rise abruptly from the river, on the other, vast stretches of prairie, dotted here and there with patches of timber, but it looks wild, and makes me think of savages. Our fare is getting low—some grumbling among the passengers, but I think Capt. Barrows has done well to feed us as he has. We are called the "happy family," and Capt. Barrows says father should be proud of his children. Bro. Sam will tease the poor old chambérmaids, and Will has made friends with the cook. Ada and Nan look after the babies.

Monday, April 7th

The boat has laid by for repairs, and we have had a chance to tread on Mother Earth, and stretch our limbs. The weather is just horrid though, so we were glad to come back to warmth and shelter.

Lib tells me that Mr. Hill has proposed to her. She says she only flirts to make her folks believe she does not care for her lover, but she says, "Mollie, *I'll love him 'till I die*," and I guess she has a true heart, for her big eyes fill with tears, when she speaks of him.

Mr. Barlow's family left us at Kansas City. The carriage was rolled away and Mr. Barlow bade me good-by very kindly, hoping I would find a kind husband *some* day. A bridal party came on the boat today. The bride was charming. She told me all about her wedding and how happy she was. Is going to California to live.

Tuesday eve, April 8th

I am suffering with headache today. I have lost my Libbie. She stopped at St. Joe. Dr. Latta and I escorted her to the hotel. We parted like old time friends, with many tears and regrets. The Dr. hoped a few tears might be shed for him. Mr. Hill kept in the background. Here we met Mr. Joe Holman, an Indianapolis friend. He says I will not enjoy Nebraska, wants father to go on to Sioux City. He introduced me to Mr. Irish, a new addition. We are getting a little weary now, as our journey is drawing to a close.

On board the boat a poor destitute creature was found today with a dying child. I started out to take up a subscription for her. Jo[e] Holman headed the list by giving $5.00. I soon raised $40 and felt repaid by her earnest gratitude. "May God bless and prosper you, my dear young lady," she said.

A poor fellow almost bled to death with hemorrhage of the nose—so with all our pleasures the sad has come, showing us that there are two sides to life, the grave and the gay, a good lesson too.

Wednesday, April 9th

We passed Brownville last night, and were delighted with the idea that we are almost at our journey's end. Uncle Chas. came on board to see us. Uncle George will meet us at Neb. City. We will be there this evening. Mr. A. has been more than attentive to Dora this whole trip. She asked me if I did not think him nice? "Yes—only his red hair and nose," which comment she did not enjoy very much, and which after all, was naughty in me to say. Mr. Purcell gave me a handsome book, as a token of remembrance. Hill looks pale and dejected, as though the arrow had lodged sure enough. Ah, Libbie! How is this?

We saw an Indian encampment today on the shore of the river—so it looks as if we were coming into the wilderness sure enough! but I am prepared for *anything*. Let come what will. I suppose I'll only have what fate has in store for me. Well, this has been a pleasant episode in my life. I have liked everyone I met. Mr. Irish asked me to correspond with him this summer, but he is too much of a stranger, and a *widower* beside. His home is in Sioux City. Holman says Mr. Irish likes me very much, and wishes him to intercede in his behalf. (I don't believe it, though.)

"Planters Hotel"
Nebraska City
Thursday, April 10th

I am rubbing my eyes to find out if this is all a dream, and if we are really landed in our new home. Looking from my window I see evidences of civilization, houses and people.

We arrived last night at sunset, two weeks from the day we started from Ind. The boat was greeted by the boom of artillery. The levee was full of people, mostly men and boys. Among the first we saw, was the genial face of Uncle George, who piloted us to his hotel.

We left the "Silver Heels" with regret. Dr. Latta, Cheeny, Irish, and all of the gents came on shore to bid us good-by, Godspeed, and good wishes. I really tried to muster up a few tears for the good doctor's benefit, but failed to show much emotion. I *liked* them all. Peace to the memory of each. "While sailing o'er life's main, my bark perchance may meet with theirs again." May they have the same kind remembrance of me. I never had a better time, and Capt. Barrows said our family had made the trip more pleasant.

Nebraska City,* nice name, but not much of a city. The town proper is situated on the hill or bluffs back from the river. But few houses are built yet. We are stopping where the town was first settled, down near the river in Kearney City. This place is three years old. I hear there are churches and stores up in the other town. Here, there are nothing but rude cabins and board shanties not even plastered. I see such lots of men, but very few ladies and children. I heard one fellow shout, "Hurrah for the girls" as father marched his brood into the hotel parlor, and Mrs. Allen, our land-lady, said, "I'm glad to see the girls." She is quite gossipy, and has already told us more than we can digest in a month. She says the place is full of gamblers, topers, and roughs of every description, and we will have to be very discreet. So I suppose we will hardly dare poke our noses outside the door for fear of contamination.

We are anxious to find a place to live. There seem to be no empty houses. Father and Uncle George are looking around. The children are delighted to be on "terra firma" again. The weather is cool, and the wind blows. They say it blows all the time, but I am too tired to bother my head about that, so good night, my Journal.

Friday, April 11th

This morning after breakfast we left the children in care of the girls, and Father, Mother, and myself started house hunting. After a vigorous search of three hours, which seemed to be composed of more than sixty minutes each, and tramping over several quarter sections of land, apparently we were compelled to take a small dilapidated log house with one small room and a three-cornered kitchen

* Nebraska City, established in 1854 near the Missouri River at the site of Old Fort Kearny, was an important port of Nebraska Ter-ritory. Its position as an eastern terminal for overland freighting made it a rival of the capital city, Omaha.

directly across the street, which we had supposed was used for a stable, at the very modest rent of fifteen (15) dollars a month, and were congratulated on securing *that,* as there is not a vacant habitation in either town. I suppose the next poor emigrants will have to live out of doors. I shall never forget the looks of dismay, when our new home was pointed out to the family. "Not that!" "Not there!" was pathetically uttered by the girls. Bro. Will threw himself upon the floor and said "he would never live in a stable." Father tried to look cheerful, but I could see the tears in Mother's eyes, and *I,* well, *I* have started out to be a heroine, a *brave, brave* girl, and I said "it would be jolly." (I did not *think* so.) But we must make the best and not get discouraged at the start.

After dinner we moved our baggage across to our new abode, the observed of all observers. To come to this! after all the style and pleasure of our trip. Well, it *was* humiliating, at least.

We cannot get a piece of furniture in the place, and scarcely any provisions. We all went to work scrubbing and digging and cleaning, had our new cook stove put up, converted our largest packing box into a table, and stood around eating our meager supper of baker's bread and coffee. Our beds are made upon the floor, the family piled promiscuously into them. My place is waiting for me, and Dora has just said, "How upon *earth* you can have the heart to sit and write I can't see." I know we should be thankful that we are all alive and well. This is only the beginning—the end may be better. So I'll say my prayers with a thankful heart tonight, acknowledging my blessings and accepting the misfortunes as belonging to mortals here below.

So let me to sleep and forget for a while, and be ready with the morning's light to be up and doing. Good night. Good night.

Sabbath eve, 13th

O, but didn't we work yesterday! and we are really trying to be cheerful. The day was beautiful and warm. I am told this is a lovely country in summer with its verdant prairies, varied flowers, and delightful atmosphere.

Our cabin is near the banks of the creek, where a grove of tall, naked trees stretch their branches toward the sky. Perhaps, when clothed in their summer foliage and the birds singing 'mid their boughs, they may suggest more of the beautiful than now.

The children are happy. The boys in cleaning up the yard have unearthed some treasures. Will has found a genuine one dollar gold piece, which has reconciled him to living in a "stable."

Uncle George is here surrounded by Mother and the girls, telling of some of his exploits. Some of his yarns about the country are pretty "far fetched" and I do wonder if they have forgotten how he loves to dwell upon the marvelous? and how he will laugh at them tomorrow for being "gulled." Father has been rambling around today. We have all kept close indoors.

I am crouched on the floor with a trunk for my writing table and the girls wonder "what I do find to write about so much." They do not understand the relation I sustain to my journal, the pleasure I take in transferring my thoughts to its pages.

Wednesday, 16th

Several days have elapsed since I made an entry in these pages. We have been very busy.

The weather continues lovely and needs but the green leaves and blooming flowers to make it seem like June. We are becoming more reconciled to our surroundings. A boat load of freight has arrived, and we now boast of two cottage bed steads, a dining table, and some chairs. We have our carpet down and lots of little trinkets we brought from home, and tonight all seem contented. There's not half the virtue in being happy when surrounded by luxuries, as when deprived of them.

Father and Uncle George have gone off to hunt land. Of course the land near by has all been taken up, and to get a place desirable, or with timber, they will have to go 25 or 30 miles away. Timber only grows in this country on the streams. We do not care how soon we leave here. Our cabin stands almost in the middle of the street, and we cannot step outside the door without being stared at by the loafers over at the hotel and saloon. We do not even like to sit by the windows to attract attention, so we content our selves with peering and peeking out at the loop holes between the logs, where the chinking has been knocked out.

We had a scare today. Will came rushing in to tell us that "Sam had fallen down the well." He had heard a terrible screeching across the street, where Sam had gone for water. When we came to investigate we found it was the braying of a lonely, hungry mule. Will thought the noise, the dying shrieks of his brother.

Someone rapped at the door today. I opened it, and there was a gentleman who informed us he "was hunting a girl," to work in his hotel. He had seen so many here he thought we would like to go out to work. With a decided toss of her head Dora told him "we had not come to *that* yet," and Miss Nan with her nose elevated at an angle of 45 degrees informed him that "when we wanted a place, we would let him know." I was more amused than insulted, and said "I thought six dollars a week pretty good wages, and if the worst came to the worst *I* might go." He bowed himself out, and after he left I could but think how nice if we could help lighten our Father's burdens. Of course, there are more ways than in going out to do housework. I feel as if we were terribly indolent. We have no work at all, hardly.

When Mother came in from her walk, the girls told how "terribly we had been insulted," and explained it all by our living in this horrid old house.

Perhaps all of this may be for our good. We have lived in the city so long and tried to keep up appearances, and would feel unhappy if we could not have this or that luxury or comfort, never thinking it all had to come through one pair of hands, or that we might help by our efforts.

April 19th

We have been treated today to a genuine Nebraska wind storm. We just don't do anything during these storms, but gouge the dust out of our eyes and ears, and wish ourselves back in civilization again.

Early this forenoon I took a little ramble up into the other town. Duly rigged in my new spring bonnet and other finery, I expected to create a sensation. It was calm when I started, but before I ascended the hill, there came a gust of wind that sent my bonnet flying and flapped my garments about my form until I looked more like a liberty pole, than the dashing belle I had started out to be, but smoothing my ruffled plumage, I went ahead, called at the three dry goods stores (and *such* stores!) At one place was a good-looking, black-eyed clerk, who left his desk, hastily jamming his pen over his ear, and came forward apparently well pleased, but alas! my feathers drooped when glancing into an 8 by 10 fly-bespeckled looking glass I discovered my bonnet hanging on the back of my head, and my raven tresses streaming down by back, my whole costume out of gear. All the result of that passing breeze. I made apologies and expressed my contempt for all such countries as Neb. but he laughed (I know he was dying to all the time) and said I would soon get accustomed to the spring winds, that summer would be *so* delightful I would forget all my annoyances. We go to church tomorrow, Dora and I.

Sabbath, April 20th

The second one spent here. The wind blew so hard we did not venture to go to church. Our neighbor Mrs. Boulware came in a while. She says if we wait for calm weather we will *never* go, or not until June, so it is some consolation to know there is a limit to the wind. So we went this evening and I was so glad we did. There was a real nice congregation.

Dick Gregory (everybody calls him "Dick") called on us this eve. He is bar 'tender at Allens Hotel. I must confess I do not feel flattered; we have not been in the habit of associating with that class of men, but he made so many excuses. He had landed here destitute and could get nothing else to do, and would, as soon as he got his board bill paid, stop it, and Mother says he has the appearance of being a good fellow, and for us to treat him well and we might encourage him to seek good company. He has been very kind to us in many ways.

Dear Father returned from his trip today, tired and hungry. He is delighted with the country and has secured 160 acres of land 30 miles from here, on the "Little Nemaha."

He will immediately take material and put us up a house, where he will establish us, and then come into the "City" and work at his trade. Carpenters and builders are in great demand here.

April 24th

Father left again on Monday for the "Little Nemaha" and after he had started there came up a wild, raging snowstorm, and now it lies deep on the ground. O! where is dear Father tonight? There are no houses near his camping place. Sweet angels care for him and bring him safely home!

"Dick" now comes in every day, is very good company when there are no others of more brilliant address to throw him into the shade.

I find my journal a great source of pleasure. I can say with perfect impunity, *any*thing about *any*body I please, but I must not be unkind or unjust to anyone. I hope I may *never*, through malice or thoughtlessness, write anything here that in after years I should be ashamed to see. I begin to think "Dick" is quite interested in one of we girls. I don't know. I don't want to be egotistical and imagine it to be myself, although I cannot help but half believe it. Ah! Richard!

Monday, 29th

I do not write *every* day, the time slips by so swiftly. I go out so little, I have nothing to write about and sometimes get weary of myself as a subject (poor forlorn creetur).

The storm has passed, the snow disappeared, and all nature seems springing into life. Groups of happy children play upon the streets, the sound of hatchet, hammer, and saw gives our little village an enterprising aspect. New buildings are springing up as if by magic. Dora has just returned from the P.O. and brought me a whole budget of letters. One from Mollie tells of her undying friendship. One from Libbie, protesting the same, and telling me she has been sick, and homesick. Also had letters from the relatives who miss us so much. It is lovely to hear from them all. "Dick" came over a while ago and proposed—(not himself, my journal) but a fishing party for tomorrow. I hail with delight the privilege of getting outside these dingy walls! Out into the pure air, under the bright sky! *Anything*—anybody—*any*where! rather than to mope down here much longer. I shall do something desperate if something does not "turn up" soon.

We *did* have a little sensation this afternoon. Uncle George brought over one of his chums, to introduce, and desires me to be particularly nice to him, as he is about the only *moral* young man in town, a perfect paragon of perfection, and I never knew one of that kind to hold out. Well, we were not "primped up" to receive company, but made the best of it, and asked Mr. Cornell to call again. I have heard that he has recently broken an engagement of marriage with Miss Pamelia Boulware, who is slowly dying with consumption. They had a lovers' quarrel. I am not very well impressed with him. Uncle George says, he never did care for Miss Boulware. It don't matter to me anyway, *who he loves* or *has* loved. I'm quite sure I shall never fall in love with *him*.

April 30th

And I so weary, I ought to be in bed. We had a long ramble, caught no fish, but gathered plenty of wild flowers, scuffed our shoes, tore our dresses, got tanned and sunburned, and were glad to get back to the old cabin again. Dick was a good escort and we really owe him something for his effort to make us enjoy ourselves.

May 1st

April is disposed of at last. Father is building our house. It is to be a hewn log cabin, in the woods. Yes! in the woods! miles and *miles* from anybody. Whatever will become of us? Father always said he does not want to lose his daughters, so perhaps this is a project to keep us. We will be a forlorn set. O! dear, O! *dear*.

We went down on board the "Silver Heels" on its second trip up the river. Capt. Barrows invited us to go on a pleasure trip to Omaha, but Mother said No! Since we are to take a pleasure trip into the country soon, we should be content. (Sarcastic.) There! now that's naughty for me, for I promised to be good. And I will be, too, *let come* what will.

May 5th

It has been a lovely day!

We made some calls or returned the calls of Mrs. Burnham and Hochstetter, wives of our city merchants. They are so pleasant, and seem like home folks. I told Mrs. B. that as there was but *one* good young man in town, the prospect looked gloomy enough for young company. She advised me to "set my cap" for a Mr. By Sanford, a friend of theirs, who arrived here yesterday from Indiana. I had a glimpse of him as I came out of the store today. A good-looking enough fellow. *I'll see about it.*

We went fishing again yesterday, had better luck and had a nice mess for supper. "Dick" seems grieved that we are to leave so soon—he became quite serious and nearly made a goose of himself; he was about to come to the point to propose, as we sat on the river bank fishing, but at that moment I dextrously threw my line and the hook caught his hat, which tumbled into the water, and in his efforts to rescue that, he got confused and off the track. I told him I was engaged. (I did not say to be married) but he took it that way. I have not flirted with him. On the contrary have lectured him for ever selling liquor. I have sometimes treated him real shabbily, been saucy and rude even.

I do not know whether I will *ever* love any man well enough to marry him or not. If by the time I am twenty-one, I find a good sensible fellow that won't talk silly flattery, I may transfer my maiden heart to his keeping. I don't know *what* the matter is. I so soon tire of the gentlemen, that is, if they get *too* sentimental. And I am sentimental too myself.

Sabbath, May 4th

Father came home to spend a few days with us, and get some more material for building. He took us all out for a ramble, out on the high prairie where we had a fine view of the country. The landscape was beautiful. The prairies look like a vast ocean stretching out until earth and sky seem to meet. We found many varieties of our cultivated flowers, growing in wild profusion. Father says we will love our new home. I already love the Nebraska prairies. How nice of Father to forget his weariness and try to find something to interest and please us, and we would be heartless indeed not to enter into his enthusiasm. He is a great lover of nature. Dora and I called upon the invalid young lady, Pamelia Boulware. She is very frail, and certainly not long for this world. While there Mr. Cornell came. They *seem* to be good friends. While we were there, some drunken roughs had a fight before the door. Pistols and knives were used promiscuously. Pamelia fainted, and Cornell held her in his arms until she recovered her consciousness. It seems *dreadful* to see saloons running on the Sabbath day, and I said, "I *never could stand* it," but the folks here said, "So *we* thought, but we have got used to it." I think if people would *not* get used to such things, there would be less of it. How true that

"Vice is a monster of such frightful mien
That, to be dreaded, needs but to be seen,
But seen too oft, familiar with its face,
We pity first, endure, and then embrace."

Cornell walked home with us, said he "only came in to meet us, that he rarely ever went there," and he wanted to explain some things to me, and for me not to believe all that I heard about him and Miss Boulware. He will call tomorrow. Uncle George is determined I shall treat him nicely, and of course I will, for his sake, but must say I sort of distrust Cornell, on general principles.

Friday, May 9th

Time glides along rapidly, another week well nigh gone.

Cornell *did* come over and spend the evening. Mother and the girls like him. I can't say that I do, but have promised to go to church Sabbath morning with his lordship. Dora and I were invited to spend the evening at the hotel, where we met a number of gentlemen. We were the only ladies except Mrs. Allen. They played cards. We could not be induced to take part, altho they predicted we would soon fall into the practice, since card playing and dancing are *the* amusements indulged in here. We met a Mr. Daily from N. Y., said to be wealthy. He has the looks and bearing of a man of means and culture.

Dick walked home with us, but did not say much to *me*, only that it was a shame that we neither "danced nor played cards."

Sunday, May 11th

Mr. Cornell came, and we went to church. The church is in the other town and a good long walk. One of those "gentle zephyrs" came to waft us onward, and with it a dash of rain that completely drenched us, so all of my "primping" was for nothing and I was more impressed about my spoiled new bonnet than anything else. Cornell looked dilapidated enough, and pretended to be asleep half the time, as if he would not attract more attention that way, than if he had straightened up and looked at the preacher like a "little man." I felt like pinching him. He comes again Wednesday.

Monday, May 12th

Father has gone again, and will remain until the home is finished. Then we are to go. *That* Mr. Sanford (whom we have dubbed the "yaller mule driver" from the fact of his driving a pair of buff-colored mules) took a load of sash and flooring, and I've had a face to face encounter with him. I have heretofore only admired him from across the street, as he stops over there. They will camp out on the trip. Mr. Sanford was to furnish the coffee, and asked Father to have it prepared for him at the house, and he would call for it. We all "had a finger in the pie." Nan browned it, Dode ground it, and I made the bag to put it in. There was a dispute as to who was to receive him, and deliver it. I quietly stationed Ada at the portholes, next the street, and when she saw him start over, she gave me the signal. So, duly equipped with the bag, after a vigorous scuffle, I stood by the door until he rapped. I opened it, and while I was accounting the cost of it, and he was fumbling in his pocket for a quarter to pay for it, mischievous Nan, who was on the floor behind the door, gave me a vigorous pinch on the leg, at which I screeched and before I thought shut the door in his face. Before I could open it, and apologize, he had gone. O, mercy! but he *must* have thought me rude, and can I *ever* have the opportunity of explaining to him? O! well, if I go to the country I will probably never see him again and I don't care if I don't.

Sunday, May 18th

I hardly know *how* the week has passed, but the calendar points to Sunday again. Dora and I went to church, heard a good sermon on the uncertainty of life, and the certainty of death. The fact was brought more forcibly to my mind, as I had been called the other day

[23]

to see Miss Boulware die. For hours she lay unconscious, but revived and is better. Cornell was there, the most solicitous of all, but followed me home, to tell that he was only there in the capacity of brother, that there was no love between them. I cannot see why he should act a double part. I am sure *I* do not care for him, and his attentions to me are nothing, only, I suppose, someone to go with and perhaps to show someone that he *can!* Girls are so scarce in this town, and the only reason I go with *him* is because decent *men* are so scarce, but I won't need an escort very long. The time to leave is fast approaching, and then I'll have no place to go nor no one to take me. O! dear, the gloomy prospect ahead!

Thursday, 22nd

The weather is simply lovely. We are more than busy getting our spring sewing done. George and Cornell come over every evening. Some of the town ladies called again this week. We like Mrs. Burnham and Mrs. Hochstetter rather better than any of them. I had a good look at "Sanford" today as he lounged by the store door. He is fine looking when rigged up in his suit of black, and stove pipe hat. But mercy! I don't dare to meet him. The ladies had quite a laugh at the coffee scrape.

Well, our Father has come home. He announces the house finished, and will not return until we are ready to move. He tells us that Mr. Daily, the New Yorker, has taken the quarter section of land adjoining ours, also several other bachelors have taken land, but not one family anywhere near. Dora says Mr. Daily belongs to her, as she always expected to marry rich, and I've concluded to take the "yaller mule driver," since Mrs. Burnham is so anxious I should "set my cap" for him. She sings his praises constantly.

I had letters again from the old home. Mollie tells me

Jim Hyatt is married!! There! that is as much as a distracted lover's threats amount to. When we parted two years ago, he swore he would "*kill* himself, that he would *never, never* marry anyone else. He would *die* loving me alone"—but— "Men have died, and worms have eaten them, but not for love." He tells Mollie, he only married this girl because her name was "Mary." He would worship at a "*Mary's* shrine." For the sake of old memories, *Jim*, I hope you will be happy. I wonder if he has written *her* as much poetry as he used to inscribe to *me*. I would get it by the pound on foolscap. I only remember one verse of it all. We first met at a woodland party where catching, kissing games were played. Long after we became lovers, he wrote this verse:

"When first amid the thoughtless gay,
  Thy passing form I caught,
I little knew that *love* would play
Between our distant thought.
But O! as I conversed with thee,
The *soul* in thee displayed,
Shone 'round my heart, and over me,
Like morning sunbeams played."

Some of his lines were beautiful, and I should have preserved them.

I had a ride on horseback today. Mrs. Burnham's brother John was my escort. We dashed over the prairie and through the town. I wore Mrs. B.'s riding habit. O! it was delicious sport. I felt like a bird uncaged. I was not so proud of my escort, for "John" is one of the homeliest men I ever met, but I *did* not care for *that*. I don't like handsome men anyway—they are too vain as a general thing. (Poor John!)

I have watched with Pamelia three nights this week. She wants me constantly. Strange she should like *me*, for she knows Cornell comes to see me. I cannot understand their relation. He was there too, and watched with me, but all the time protests "he does not love her." I'm sick of him anyhow!

Last night we had a serenade. Poor Dick, altho quite snubbed of late (because he still 'tends bar) is determined to assure us of his interest, and employed the string band to give us a benefit. He thinks perhaps to reach my heart through the medium of music, since it has power to "melt a rock and split a cabbage head," I've heard it said.

The first song was "Meet me by moonlight alone," then that pathetic ballad, "Thou hast learned to love another." In this, Dick's voice rose high above the jingle, with a touching cadence, that failed to reach my heart, for I've learned to love nobody, nor he either. They sang a few more pieces, and departed. I watched their forms disappear in the midnight gloom, as I stood shivering at the loop holes.

We met at the well today (not as Jacob and Rachel, though). He asked how I liked my serenade. "O!" I said, "Dick, was that you? We thought a pack of hungry coyotes had ventured in from the prairie." He looked hurt, and it was too mean in me I know, but dear me! I've got to do *something* with him. He bothers me to death.

Friday, 23rd

I am too tired tonight to write. Guess I had too much horseback riding. Cornell came in this eve. He said, "You looked perfectly divine on horseback." (That is just what he said, silly goose!) He wants to go to church *alone* with me Sunday night. Dora has always gone with us, as I preferred it that way, but I will go, and see what he has to say. I want to give him a good sensible talking to anyway, and let him know that I *know* he is trying to flirt with me. Pamelia said she hoped I would be his friend when she is gone. I want to talk to her about dying, but she does not seem to want to talk about it, altho she knows her days are numbered. I hope she is prepared. It is sad to see her go—the only and idolized daughter, beautiful and accomplished, and so much to live for, but death spares not.

Sabbath, May 25th

The *last* one we spend in Neb. City. It has rained, and poured all day, but Cornell came duly equipped with wraps and umbrella, and *insisted* on my going to church. I wish I could enjoy the services as I used to at North St. Chapel. Every face *there* wore a smile of greeting. Here there is a formal bow and a speculative stare. O! for a good old-fashioned handshake! Cornell acts very sanctimonious, but is not a church member. I let the hymn book fall upon his corns in church, which 'roused him somewhat out of his solemn mood.

We did not have any "talk," it rained so hard. It was all we could do to get home, and perhaps the cold, chilling rain dampened his ardor, or maybe his corns ached, but he wants me to take a walk tomorrow evening when he proposes to give me an entire and full history of his and Pamelia's engagement and present relations. It will be his last chance, for we leave on Wednesday.

Tuesday, 27th

I will only add a few lines tonight. Since yesterday morning we have been busy preparing for our change of residence, doing a lot of cooking, for we have to "camp out." It is nice and warm since the rain and we will have a nice trip. Cornell came, and we took a walk down by the river side alone. He told me a lot of stuff about his and Pamelia's "mistaken affection." That they had vowed to be brother and sister, and that she had advised him to marry me, at which he duly proposed. I told him I did not believe him, to go back to his old sweetheart and cheer her dying hours, that I *knew* he had been flirting all the time, perhaps to wound her. He looked surprised but murmured, "Time will prove me to have been sincere," and here, and now, I bid farewell to this hero, and wait for another to come upon the stage.

My next talk will be in the wildwoods of our new home, "Little Journal."

Our few neighbors came in to say good-by. I went to take my last farewell of Pamelia. She looked at me so curiously. Poor girl, I shall never see her again, and hope in some way I have helped her to die more easily, for I *know she loves Cornell.*

CHAPTER TWO

Homesteading on the Little Nemaha

June 5, 1857—August 20, 1857

"Little Nemaha" — June 5th

  On this lovely afternoon, under the spacious shadow of an old elm tree by our cabin door, I am seated with my book upon my knee, to give the details of the past few days, my Journal dear, to thee.

  By sunrise on Wednesday morning, the wagons were packed, and we had started upon the road. Father, Mother, and the smaller children rode with Mr. Hemphill, a tow-headed delegate from the settlement (and if he is a specimen of the fellows out there, oh! deliver us, sweet fate, deliver us!) We girls rode with Mr. Henry Brown, a Neb. City gent and a nice travelling companion!

  There was not even a *shadow* of regret at leaving our abode, altho Cornell stood on the corner looking so forlorn. Willie had his pack of stray dogs ready, but when told that he could not take all he selected his favorite, a big yellow mastiff, and tied him behind the wagon. The deserted pups whined as they were tied to the fence posts, and old "crazy John," one of his pets, dug the corner of his eye with his dirty coat sleeve, and gave the boy an affectionate farewell. The love of the poor dogs, and the affection of demented John was worth something to my generous, friendly brother, who makes friends always with the unfortunate.

It was cool and cloudy all day. The prairies were soft and green as velvet carpets, the atmosphere laden with the perfume of a thousand flowers.

We travelled 14 miles before stopping, over a road sometimes level as a floor, then up and down, through gullies and ruts, through tangled grass and muddy sloughs, until we reached the cabin of Mr. McWilliams and the only one to be seen. On the trip, here and there as we came along we could see small claim shanties, where people had taken up land, but not a tree or shrub in sight until we reached the first branch of the Nemaha.

We borrowed a table and had our dinners in the "bachelors hall." During the two hours nooning rambled through the woods. It is refreshing to come to these patches of timber, after travelling for hours over a treeless plain.

Dora made a beautiful bouquet of wild flowers and, hunting up an old tin can, left it on the table in the cabin. She thought it too bad to leave so many "flowers to blush unseen and waste their fragrance on the desert air."

Mr. Brown thought it "casting pearls before swine," and thought the flowers sadly out of place in that dirty hole, but who knows what sweet memories this little act may awaken even in the heart of rough, uncouth Mr. Mc-Williams.

Leaving the Nemaha, we were again on the prairie, on, on, with no travelled road, and apparently no object in view.

We had planned to make the trip to our home that day, and whose line of timber was visible in the twilight only several miles away. One of the horses gave out and we lost our track in the grass. Father lost his bearings, and we were compelled to stop for the night. We were near a slough of brackish water, warm and muddy, and had to use the dry weeds for fuel to boil our kettle for tea. It tasted deliciously, the hot steaming beverage, but when we came to use the rest of the water for our dishes, we found the dishrag had been boiled up in it, and that accounted for the rich flavor of the tea. "Campers" must expect such things, the men say. Mother tried to get rid of her supper by retching herself almost to death, but I held on determinedly to mine, after having so hard a time to get it.

By the light of dried weeds we made our beds on the ground beneath the wagons. The teamsters laid on the grass with nothing to shelter them.

The sensation of sleeping out of doors was queer enough, *out* under the twinkling stars, in the bosom of the broad prairie, *sounds* romantic enough but we did not speculate about it and were glad to close our weary eyes in sleep, and dreams.

About one o'clock, the wind came up, the horses were uneasy, and Father thought we had better be travelling on, as a storm was coming, and the rain is something dreadful on the plains with no place of shelter.

Hitching up in a hurry, they piled us into the wagons again, and we took up our line of march.

But where were we going? Darkness was over all, no light, no road! Father made a torch and finally found the track but so faint he had to *keep* hunting it. We sometimes stopped entirely, until the voice of our guide would hallo for us to "come ahead."

As morning approached, the clouds passed away and our fears were allayed, the storm spirit no doubt pitying our helpless condition.

Soon the bright face of morning peeped o'er the eastern horizon, when we again came in view of the timber surrounding our home. It gave new hope to us, and new speed to the horses; and we soon reached the woods. I never felt more relieved and thankful, now that we had come through safely and were coming to a home of our own once more.

The sunrise was glorious! the trees full of singing birds, ringing out a welcome. Soft zephyrs floated o'er us, bright flowers gave out their perfume, and all nature was glad. Father had named the place "Hazel Dell," and we christened it by singing that sweet song. And such a chorus as went up from those lumbering wagons! Birds stopped their carols to listen, and festive chipmunks flew from their hiding places, bewildered with the noise. And when we reached the cabin joyful hurrahs! resounded long and loud.

It was not long before the cook stove was set out and a bounteous breakfast was served, delicious coffee made from the clear, sparkling water of the Nemaha, with no taint of stewed dishrags to spoil the effect. Even Father and Mother were as gleeful as the children, for a while.

The "Nemaha" here is about 20 ft. wide, a clear, sparkling stream where myriads of tiny fish sport, and whose banks are overhung with creeping vines and flowers.

Great elm trees grow on its margin, their branches intertwining, forming an arch overhead. The foliage is dense, and such an air of quiet seclusion as surrounds the place! is restful at least.

The little boys have been chasing squirrels and finding all sorts of curiosities in the woods, and are wild with delight.

Our cabin is of hewn logs, a good-sized room of 20 ft. square, two windows and one door, and a clapboard roof. We are quite settled and look cozy, and if there is not room enough inside there is plenty out of doors, yes! plenty!!

Mother hardly enters into extacies. She no doubt realizes what it is to bring a young rising family away from the advantages of the world. To *me*, it seems a glorious holiday, a freedom from restraint, and I believe it will be a blessing to we girls. We were getting too fond of style, too unhappy not to have the necessary things to carry it out.

The novelty of this life may wear off in time, but I hope I will have the good sense and judgement to make the very best of our circumstances.

Uncle George and Mr. Daily are keeping bachelors hall across the creek. They say, no more quiet for them, no more morning snoozes. It seems when Father left we were handed over to their tender care. I informed them I could care for myself. Mr. Daily has donned his backwoods garb, and does not look so awe inspiring as he did the evening we met him at Mrs. Allen's. Uncle George will hardly forgive me for not accepting Cornell.

"Sabbath in the Woods," June 8th

I have been on the rampage for three days, exploring the woods, catching fish, and helping in the garden, for altho late, Mother says, we must have some vegetables.

We *all* seem content. Even *Mother* has caught the inspiration and lost her care-worn look and, Mother dear, we will try and make you happy yet.

Home! Sweet Home! There's no place so dear, no charm so sacred. Well may angels be supposed to linger within your walls, and shed within their incense of heavenly blessings. This sanctuary of domestic happiness, this tie that binds our hearts in sacred compact from whence arises the genial affections of our better natures. I feel that I do not do all that I might to make the home happy. I am full of good resolves tonight to *do* better and *be* better than ever before. How lovely it is tonight! I have no church in which to worship, no stereotyped sermon to listen to, *but* I can look around and see God's beautiful creations and find a sermon in stones, and trees and flowers.

I can sit here in the mellow evening's light, so still, so quiet, and commune with the angel spirits that sometimes come to me. They seem to tell me in soft, sweet whispers not to doubt, that this life, so full of cares and perplexities, is not all. There is a life beyond this vale of tears, and trials are but to prepare us for that life, where no sorrow comes.

I want to be *good*. I *try* to be, too, but some way, I fall into many grievous errors. Perhaps my light frivolous nature was given me to help those differently constituted. I'll try to keep from going into any foolish excesses. May the sweet angels watch over me, and keep me in the memory of the vows I make tonight.

Wednesday, 12th

A week in our new home already. One would suppose time would hang heavily upon our hands, but no. We all work in the garden. With the help of Mr. Daily and George we have quite a patch. The soil is light and loamy and easily prepared. I never made garden before, but then, I'm prepared to do anything. Nan cares for the babies, and Addie keeps the house filled with lovely flowers. Mother has an easy time. We do not allow her to do much work. She has been an invalid much of her life, and I do believe with lessened burdens and pure air and quiet, she will become stronger. We are all as well as we can be, eat and sleep well.

Father returned to the city with Mr. Brown the day after we got here. He will come home occasionally. He has work, and needs to keep employed, and I often feel guilty to think he is working hard and we are almost idle. With our increased health and appetites it will take hard work to keep the "wolf from the door." That reminds me that we may have to *fight* to keep the wolf from the door ourselves, for the woods are full of them, or the *prairies* are. The family are horrified because I sleep with my head outside the door. The nights are suffocating, and I lie on the floor, with the door half open and my head on the threshold. I suppose it is hardly wise, for there are rattle snakes around here, altho we have not seen any yet.

June 15th

It has been a hot day, awfully hot. We were surprised today by a call from "Dick," the veritable Dick, who has scented us to our wildwood home. He was on his way to Tecumseh, the county seat, and came ten miles out of his way to deliver a message from Father. We gave him his dinner and sent him on his way. He is going to leave the country. I'm glad.

June 20th

Had another call today, a black-eyed lawyer from Neb. City, Mr. Mann. He had walked, and was very tired, besides having had an encounter with a rattle snake, and had the rattles as a trophy of his bravery.

I said, "O! Mr. Mann, describe a rattle snake. I never saw one." He began by saying, "It is as long as a common stick, dark in color, and has a bunch of rattles on the end of its—" then a blank—filled by his taking his handkerchief and wiping the perspiration from his "man-ly" brow. I meekly suggested, "On the end of its tail, Mr. Mann." "Yes! Yes!" he gasped, "on the end of its t-a-i-l."

I might have said "narrative," since he was too modest to use the more vulgar expression. He brought a bundle of letters and some messages from Father—one from Cornell, begging me to reconsider my decision.

After Mr. Mann left we went to the creek to bathe. We have a lovely bathing hole, and some improvised bathing suits, a secluded place, where we have grand sport splashing in the water. The boys have a swimming hole, and I have almost learned to float.

We were called to the house to meet Mr. Will Hemphill, our "tow-headed" teamster, who, with his brother, has a claim nearby. He was rigged in a white cotton suit with "yaller" necktie and huge straw hat and looked "blonder" and *blander* than ever and, but for the twirling of the hat, I don't know what he would have done with his hands. He stayed, and lingered, until I exhausted my powers of entertainment, and finally said "guessed he'd go but would come again soon." No sooner had he left than Daily and Uncle George came in, full of fun, with "O! ho! had a beau!" and come to find out they had persuaded him to come and ask for my company, telling him that I had fallen in love with him on the trip from town. He was goose enough to believe it.

Then I understood why all the folks had left the room, and we alone. I suppose I must have *awed* him—I certainly tried to. I'll be even with those boys yet, if it takes me all summer!

Sunday, June 21st

This morning after we were all "dressed up" (which we do every Sunday morning as regularly and religiously as if we were in civilization), two strange gentlemen came, announcing themselves as neighbors, had been invited by the boys to be neighborly. They evidently came to spend the day, and would be our guests at dinner. We had about run ashore for provision, not having had an installment since we moved. Having no milk, no butter, eggs, nor vegetables, it seemed a gloomy prospect, for those that wished to be hospitable. Mother, who feels our circumstances more keenly with her proud English spirit, took the babies and fled to her retreat in the woods, where she often goes to gain her equilibrium. I knew our bachelor friends would expect a square meal, so as I'm chief cook anyway, I knew the honors devolved upon me, so put my wits to work accordingly. We have put up a brush kitchen at the end of the house, as it grew so hot we could not cook indoors, so leaving the girls to entertain the gentlemen, now increased to four by Uncle George and Mr. Daily, I started my fire and began to *think up* my bill of fare. I had a few days before found a large bush of wild gooseberries, almost large enough for use. The boys soon gathered them and by theirs and Ada's help they were soon picked over. I had no lard, so fried out some fat meat, made some pie crust and baked a pie. Then made a cake using my shortening, and vinegar and saleratus to make it light, took my dry bread and dipped it in batter and fried it nice and brown, floured and fried my fat meat, had a good cup of coffee, and a dish of the stewed gooseberries.

In the meantime the girls had set the table in our best appointments, with a snowy linen cloth, nice glassware, and our handsome dishes, and when all was ready, they hunted up Mother, and when she came in she looked surprised enough, but *I*, as cool as a cucumber as tho we were accustomed to such a "spread." The men ate with a relish that corresponded with their verdict, that "it was the best meal they had had in the country." We are expecting a load of provision, a cow, and some chickens soon and hope to be ready for the *next* emergency. The folks gracefully yield to me.

Tuesday, 23rd

What should I do without my journal! I have Mother and the girls to talk with, but I cannot talk as freely to them as to this, my "bosom friend." I might be reproved and not always appreciated.

I am a little homesick tonight. I am thinking of Mollie dear! and of the many dear friends of the past. My life is not what I pictured it a year ago. My airy castles have tumbled, and I feel *so* far away. The rain is falling in torrents, thunder peals and lightnings flash. The wind moans thro these tall trees a requiem to joy, but there, Mollie, yours not to be blue.

I'll hie me to bed and forget in slumber all that is calculated to make me sad. Good-night! my Journal.

Sabbath eve, June 27th [?]

The hands of the clock, even now, point to bed-time, but I generally take time to write, when all are asleep, and by the dim light of my candle scribble my conflicting thoughts, for they are sometimes sad, and sometimes gay. Life is full of smiles and tears.

It is a pleasant sight to look about our cabin. The boys are spread out upon their pallets on the floor, enjoying the unbroken slumber of perfect health. Baby Charlie lies on Mother's breast, looking as pure and sweet as a cherub dropped from the skies, his night dress thrown from his shoulders, exposing his perfect limbs, his golden hair parted from his bonny brow, his dark eyelashes kissing his rosy cheek. A sweet smile dimples his mouth, as though sweet angels were whispering him stories of their heavenly home. Denty is sweetly slumbering, while Mother softly sleeps, a while free from care. My sisters sweetly dream the hours away.

I do try to feel that it is all for the best to be away off

here. I can see and feel that it chafes Mother's spirit. It worries her to think that we are in such straitened circumstances, but my father had to make a change. His idea is to secure this land for the benefit of his boys, who will soon be able to care for it. If the country would only fill up, if there were only schools or churches, or even some society. We do not see a woman at all. All men, single, or bachelors, and one gets tired of them. Then it is unpleasant for Father to be gone from home. *That* seems to discourage Mother. He will be home now in a few days to make us a visit. We will make home happy for him.

June 29th

Father came home last night with Mr. Hochstetter's family. Mr. H, is to take a piece of land a mile above us. They were brought out by my hero of the "coffee scrape," Mr. Byron N. Sanford. They are with us until their cabin can be fixed up some. They came to live on the place long enough to secure it. We are delighted to have a family near us, to see a live woman again.

I have become a little acquainted with "By," as they call him. I have made it all right about shutting the door in his face. Today while mixing up my bread he came and planted himself directly before me. I felt embarrassed and asked him to leave, but he would not and kept on watching me. I think I never made such a mess in my life, with a batch of dough. I felt like daubing it into his whiskers (which, by the way, are splendid), and I find he has pleasant blue eyes.

It is refreshing to meet a fellow like him after seeing so many flattering fops. It is wonderful how free and easy people become in this country.

I would once have thought it too presuming for a gent to make himself so much at home on so short an acquaintance. Our floor is piled full of beds tonight. The men-folks have gone to Daily's cabin to sleep.

June 30th

Father and Mr. Sanford went to town. Mr. S. comes back in a few days with a load of provision. Mr. Daily and George have come to board. It gives us something to do. Daily advanced Father some money to buy chickens and a cow. We got them today, and are happy, as far as that goes. Well, yes, happy anyhow. We might as well be.

I killed a rattle snake today, a huge one, with eleven rattles. But for its timely warning I might not be here to tell the tale. I was in my bare feet going down the path to the creek, and almost stepped upon it. The "rattles" are preserved as a trophy and his defunct snakeship hung on the limb of a tree, a warning to all of its kind. Only to think of being out here among wild cats, wolves, and snakes!!

Mr. Daily is very attentive to Dora, and I believe she likes him. We are rather antagonistical at times. We argue too much, both too positive. Mr. Daily is smart. He has fine eyes that I admire, is about 40 years old, but he is not a man that I would ever *fall in love* with. But he is a generous friend, and Father's brother Mason, and makes himself necessary to us.

July 2nd

"My" Mr. Sanford came out today, bringing that load of provision. We find plenty of wild berries through the woods and will have quantities of fruit later. I don't know *why* I should call Mr. Sanford "mine" unless because the folks have assigned him to me, and because I like him. He is the cutest fellow I ever met. Father has come back to spend the Fourth. The weather is intensely hot. We almost live out of doors, gypsies that we are.

July 5th

The heat is intense. The glorious "Fourth" has passed. The little brothers tried to make it seem like "Fourth of July back home" by marching to the tune of "Yankee Doodle," with tin pans as drum accompaniment, with flags and banners of red flannel. Will was disgusted because we did not all join in the procession, and only comforted to know that we were preparing dinner, and by Mr. Daily firing his revolver. So "Hazel Dell" can boast of a *demonstration*. Mr. Daily had sent for a box of lemons and some confectionery. We had baked up some good things and with Mr. Hochstetter and Sanford as guests, had our dinner under the trees. We sang the national songs, and had a nice time.

One year ago tonight I went with dear old Court Whitsit to witness a grand display of fireworks at Indianapolis. I wonder if he thinks of me! and I wonder if I might not have in time learned ,to like him as much as he did me!? O, well, *that* chance has gone. Wonder if I'll *ever* have another anyway, or will I settle down here and never marry at all? I shall not worry, for I suppose I will do just what *fate* has in store for me, as *fate* controls everything.

Sunday, July 6th

Father has returned to town and "Sanford" remains a week to recruit those precious mules. He takes his pay for hauling in board. *We* do not object, nor do "Urbana" and "Sidney." The dear buff creatures lay back their long ears and wade into the delicious grass. "By" hitched them up today and took us up to Hochstetter's, where we had been invited to dinner. We came near being fooled out of our visit, too.

Before starting, Addie and I went over the creek to

milk the cow. I am the only one on the premises brave enough to milk her, and she has upset *me* several times.

She was late coming up today and we were ready dressed to go. The only way to cross the creek without going thro the water is on a peeled cottonwood log which lays across from bank to bank, and which proves treacherous, too, sometimes.

We had started across on our way home, *I* with my pail and Ad with a pitcher of "strippings," when over turned the log and we went floundering into the water, pails, pitcher, milkmaids, and all. Addie screamed and I laughed, but we were both completely drenched, and lost our milk. Mr. Sanford and the family rushed to the rescue, and escorted the dripping mermaids to the house.

Mrs. Hochstetter does not like living here. Their cabin is so small that we had to stay outside while she cooked the dinner. She sent "By" and I to gather gooseberries, but some way, we did not find many. It was not half so romantic doing that as to sit 'neath overhanging vines and talk and gaze at each other.

He showed me the picture of his sweetheart (I suppose as a warning). I like him *very* much. He says he is not engaged to this "Maria," but why does he carry her image next to his heart! She is very plain looking, but he says she is good, so he measures people by their worth more than looks, and dear me! I'm afraid I haven't either.

We got back to dinner without the berries, and when we said there weren't any, we were teased some. By seemed to like it, but I don't know whether I did or not. We came home in the cool of the evening and By went with me to milk the cow, unromantic as it was.

Tuesday, July 8th

Daily and Sanford went off on a trip today to hunt up something, about some land. Dora and I went up a couple of miles above on the creek, where we heard Mr. and Mrs. Allen, some of our "Silver Heel" friends, had located. We were mutually surprised at finding ourselves neighbors. For fear of snakes, we wore Daily's and Uncle George's boots. We came up unobserved and sat down back of the house to exchange them for our shoes, when Mrs. Allen, seeing our black heads underneath the window, thought we were Indians, and it took some time to convince her to the contrary, and have her open the door. She will not be reconciled to this frontier life and will soon leave Mr. Allen to enjoy it alone (poor soul).

Mr. Allen looks as if he had a hard time, and no doubt *she* suffers too, for she does not *sleep* for fear of wild beasts and Indians. It is more lonely than where we are, and they have no children. Mr. Allen brought us home in an ox team by moonlight. We had a jolly ride and cheered her up ever so much, I hope. She thinks if she were where *I* was she would be happy, and I fear if I were where *she* was I would not be. Some people have the faculty of making others miserable. By and I took another hunt for gooseberries yesterday. Of course we *found* some, and had a good visit besides. He became quite confidential, and told me some of his history, of a recent loss of his property by fire, and the greater loss of friends by death. He has recently buried his mother, who died of cancer of the breast, and was a great sufferer. He told me how she died in his arms and how much he loved her, and I know he is good. The tears stood in his blue eyes.

He can be funny, as well as serious. Last night he said something about being in the Mexican war, how, wounded, he was left to die on the battlefield, and when he had us all ready to weep, he said, "You girls wanted a 'story' and this is an 'all-fired' big one, for I never saw Mexico."

Uncle Chas. from Brownville is here. He comes in the interest of a town company, and we are to have a town site, anyway. We had a wild strawberry shortcake for tea, and Uncle thinks we are pleasantly situated, and that Father has done a wise thing to secure this quarter section of land.

July 27th

Near three weeks have passed without my writing. I had no ink. Beside, we have been so busy. The weather is stifling. We have had some men with teams breaking up land. Another year, Father will try farming.

Nothing of interest has transpired. Occasionally we have had to entertain travellers, all men, not one solitary female but Mrs. Hochstetter and Mrs. Allen have we seen, but we hear of a family only a mile below, where there is a married lady and single sister. We will hunt them up at once.

Daily is too sweet to Dode for anything. Things begin to look serious (and Mother does too). Mother thinks as *I* do that he has a "history," and *yet* he is like a brother, so kind and thoughtful. Uncle George has gone to Brownville to be with Uncle Chas.

About the only employment we have now, outside of our housework, is to help destroy the potato bugs that are eating up the vines—that, and playing in the creek to keep cool. We are tanned awfully, and look a little rough, I know.

The little boys have been for sport besmearing their faces with the black mud that settles in the bottom of the creek. We discovered it took the tan and sunburn off. We hailed the discovery with delight, for here was a cosmetic, so available and "cheap as dirt." So one day last week we donned our bathing suits, and sneaked off to the creek, doing our heads up in cotton handkerchiefs, to save our hair from contact, plastered our faces thickly over with the black mud, and sat on the bank for it to take effect. I was called to the house to bake the bread, and had to clean my face, but "Dode" thought while she had her coat of armor on it would be a good time to pick off the potato bugs, and she went to work. She was so intent she didn't see a gentleman ride up to the door. I could have given the signal, but did not. He was inquiring the road to Tecumseh. I told him I'd call the girl, and halloed, "You, Topsy! come here." Supposing I was fooling as we had been doing all the afternoon, she raised her head, rolled her eyes, and made a horrid grimace. Just then she spied the stranger. It did not take long for her to scale the creek bank and disappear. I did not explain, altho the man looked mystified. When she came in later, she was madder than anything, and altho we have found ourselves a few shades whiter I think we'll not try it again soon.

Mr. Hochstetter has a younger brother, "Mr. Joe," who lately came to see them. Mrs. H. thought it the thing to bring him down to get acquainted.

We were cleaning house and dressed for the occasion, with as little of the superfluous as possible. I was without a waist, my head done up in a dirty hand towel, and Dora even in a worse plight than I. The first intimation I had of their presence was a rap on the door I was cleaning on the inside, and opening it, there they stood!! I could not run, but Dode leaped through the back window, carrying a part of the sash with her. In the introduction that followed Joseph stumbled over the pail of hot soapsuds, the whole thing was so funny that we all laughed, and when he was invited to step out of doors until we could be made more presentable, he did so with alacrity. Mrs. H. had been telling him what nice girls we were, and no doubt he was disenchanted. We got up a good dinner, and all passed off pleasantly. I find that it is a good way to equalize things.

Mrs. H. will leave in a few days, so we will miss our neighbor, and no danger of "Joe" leaving his heart.

August 1st

Another week without writing. We are very busy gathering and putting up berries and currants. Our barrel of sugar is doing us good service. It quite compensates us for the lack of many things to have this wild fruit.

We had planned to have a long ramble thro the woods today, but I was cheated out of it by an unforeseen accident. The "cow" was late again, and I had to go to milk her. Being in a hurry, I did not go down to the crossing log, but pulling off my shoes and stockings I waded over. When I came back one of my shoes was missing, and the united efforts of the family failed to find it. The "pup" that sat so innocently nearby could no doubt have told us, but he only wagged his tail and gave a dogged smile at our consternation. They were all I had, and I shall have to go with one foot unshod, until we can get another pair from town.

August 10th

Our town site is established. It is called "Helena." A frame building has been erected to be used as general store and post office. Two young men have charge of it, Mr. Bennet and Mr. Favorite. They board with us. They spend their evenings here, are both excellent singers, so we have no time to be lonesome or mope.

One of the first letters coming thro the office was from Grandfather Dorsey, telling us that he was preparing to come to Nebraska. "By" is out again. He has taken up land 3 miles above us, and will be here often now, making his improvements. I am teased about him until I wonder if I do not care a little for him? for an allusion to him even makes my cheeks burn and my heart beat quicker.

He gets here generally after dark. He won't hurry up those lazy mules. One night I thought I heard him hallo!

from across the creek. Jumping from the bed, I put my
head outside the door and said, " 'By,' is that you?" Again
I heard, "Ter hoo! Ter hoo," and felt sheepish enough,
when I discovered it to be a night owl's screech. I thought
to creep slyly back to bed, but the folks had heard me, and
the joke was too good to keep. When "By" came again
Mr. Daily had to tell it at the breakfast table, and I suppose
I shall never hear the last of it. "By" thought I had paid a
high compliment to his manly? voice.

He walked with me last night a mile down the creek to
call on the Campbell family, our new neighbors. We found
them very entertaining and were induced to stay quite late
Father, getting uneasy, started out to hunt us, and some
way I felt sheepish to be patrolled home. We were coming
very slowly along the path by the soft silver moonlight,
and Father's sudden appearance and reproof for staying so
late rather spoiled the romance of the thing. Mrs. Campbell's sister is very shy, and so quiet. I fear she won't prove
much of an addition to our society. She is Miss Philpot by
name. They tried to be real nice, but I can see they are not
our kind of people. Today is Mr. By's birthday. He is 12
years older than I. Mr. Daily has been in town for a while.
I should think he would leave here.

August 20th

Two weeks' silence again, my little book. 'Tis not
because I take less interest, but because I have to work a
little more. We are obliged to keep the people that drive
up here at nightfall. It is just half-way between Neb. City
and Beatrice, and going each way they stop here. They
could stop 6 miles either side, but they say we are the best
people to stop with. One of the older gentlemen that
stopped the other day said "the Beatrice boys would break
their necks to reach this place." Well, it is company, and
helps along with our expenses. It is a little hard upon me,

as I take the burden of the cooking. Nan says, "It is a poor house that cannot afford *one* lady," and she shirks a little, but of course she is younger, and being sick so much we have spoiled her. Ada is my good angel. She is always with me. In our tramps gathering fruit she is by me, dear affectionate child! I love her so! Nan is the mischief of the family. Dora is a little precise, and Nan is never so happy as when getting her embarrassed, or playing some joke upon her. There were several of the Beatrice boys here one night. Anna entertained them while we other girls cooked the supper. They asked her to give our different names, so that they could address us separately. She said, "There's Mollie, 'Sophronia Ellen,' Ada, and myself (Anna)." The next time Dora came into the room one of the gents called her Miss "Sophronia Ellen." Dora's look of dismay (she dotes on the name of Dora) and immediate contradiction was amusing, but somewhat embarrassing, until *I* came to the rescue and explained that it was one of her sister's pet names. They all laughed, and she has been called by that name for some time.

I have had a queer experience that I must relate. I had gone to bed one night, but could not sleep. My father was constantly in my mind. I seemed to feel that he was coming home, altho he had only left two days before, and his visits home only occur every two or three weeks, as it is so far, and he generally walks, as it is too expensive to hire a conveyance. So the idea of his coming directly back was too absurd for anything, but still the impression that he was coming, and would be with me soon was so strong that I finally got up and started a fire. It was not so cold, but I was shivering for some cause. Mother awakened and asked what on earth I was doing, and when I told her I was looking for Father, she thought I was losing my senses. Hardly aware of what I *was* doing, I ground and made some coffee. Mother was about to get up and shake me, when we heard the dogs bark, then voices, and soon Father was at the door. He was accompanied by Mr. Sanford and a Mr. Holden, whom they had brought out to get land. Father was so anxious to get good neighbors that he stopped his work to come with him. They did not start from town until dark, and travelled most of the night.

Mr. Holden is a spiritualist and readily accounted for it all by saying I was a "medium." I hope if I am to be controlled by any spirit, it will be for good, but I don't believe in spiritualism as I have heard it. Only I know I have strong impressions sometimes, something I hardly understand.

Our home was thrown into a state of intense excitement this morning by Sam, our dear, good brother, being bitten by a rattle snake. In picketing out a young calf, the reptile struck him on the finger three times. Addie came screaming to the house as white as a sheet, Sam following with the dead snake, saying, "I killed it anyhow," and too brave to appear frightened. We are miles from a doctor, and had no remedies, only the simple ones that occurred to us.

Mother hurriedly bandaged his arm from the shoulder down. We applied saleratus. Then I thought of the drawing qualities of the black mud in the creek, so the poor young-one was taken down there and his arm and hand completely buried in it.

He had sucked the wound himself at first, but it swelled some, and he turned all sorts of spots and colors, was frightfully sick at his stomach, probably as much from our dosing him on everything we could think of. Father was away, of course. In time we could see that all danger was averted for the present, and O! what a relief. Poor Mother was perfectly prostrated after the fright was over. She sometimes feels wicked to think she is so far away from all help with her family. But it cannot be helped now. I am so thankful that I am endowed with nerve and strength of character to help take care of the family. Of course I suffer from excitement as much as any of the rest, but I seem to always know what to do, and have the nerve to do it. I feel after all that we have been very fortunate out here. A kind Providence is caring for us. We are only *one* family of the many that are settling up a new country, and some of our experiences are and will be of great benefit to us in after years, I hope. The wild outdoor life strengthens our physical faculties, and the privations, our powers of endurance. So that we do not degenerate mentally, it is all right; Heaven help us all.

CHAPTER THREE

Hazel Dell

September 1, 1857—April 15, 1858

September 1st

The first day of autumn. The weather is now delightful. Wild plums are ripening and we have good times. We have some late garden truck, and live well enough.

Last week we had two strange gents from Chicago, Mr. Vincent and Mr. Tucker, hunting for land. They came to the city of Helena expecting accommodations, and being disappointed, they were sent here. Mr. Tucker has bought Mr. Daily's land and will remain here, while Vincent leaves in disgust. He was nice though, and showed his gallantry while here. One bad rainy morning I took my pail and started to milk the cow. He thought it dreadful for a young lady to go out in such a storm and particularly to *have* to do the milking, and insisted on doing it himself. I knew very well "Boss" would not allow a strange man to come near her, but said he might go and help me. When we got to the crossing log, that miserable treacherous log! I, so accustomed to it, crossed in safety, but Vincent had hardly started before off he went into the creek. Of course I laughed, and he did too, but picked himself up and waded the rest of the way. He was wet to the skin, his shoes full of water, but he took them off, determined to follow me. We found the cow a little ways from the bars. I begged him to keep out of sight, but he "would like to see the cow that could scare him." "Boss" stood quietly until he started toward her, when down went her head and up went her heels, and—well, he did not wait to see *what* next, but scaled the bars at one leap, and gave up the job to me. He did look pitiful as he stood with dripping clothes, bare-headed and barefooted in the drizzling rain, no doubt wishing me in Guinea or Halifax for getting him into such a scrape. We got back to the house alive, and everybody laughed, of course. He took it coolly, got some dry clothes and slippers, and sat around to "cool off" and get warm. He cleaned his shoes and put them in the stove oven to dry, and then forgot them. While getting supper we wondered where the smell of burnt leather came from, when Vincent rushed frantically and drew forth his shrivelled, worthless shoes. He was good natured through it all, and gallant enough to say that he would go through the same again, for so good-looking a young lady.

But he had to walk thirty miles to the city in those slippers, and probably he repented before he went very far. (I would.)

September 15th

We have had a rainy, disagreeable week. Time will "drag its slow lengths along" when we have to be housed, but this is only a prelude to the long winter that is coming. We contrive every means for enjoyment, as we have to depend entirely upon our own resources. It seems the "cow" is the most prominent character in this Journal. The most of my adventures are connected with her. During the bad weather she strayed away, and we were several days without milk. Yesterday we heard the tinkle of her bell in the woods, but the boys failed to locate her, so rather than let her get away again, I started out. It occurred to me how much easier I could get through the tangled underbrush if I were a man! and without letting anyone know of my project, I slipped out into the back shed, and donned an old suit of Father's clothes, pulled on an old cap over my head and started on my pilgrimage. I was prowling thro the bushes calling, "Co, Boss, co, Boss, co," singing the "Farmer Boy," feeling secure that no men folks were around. Coming out from a thicket of underbrush to a clear spot, what was my consternation to emerge into a camp of men, who were quietly seated on the ground eating their breakfast! I could not scream nor faint as that feminine resource would certainly betray me, but thought "discretion the better part of valor" and that "he who runs away will live to fight another day," and the way I travelled through those woods to the house was a caution.

I intended to have had some sport when I came back by fooling the girls, but now all I thought of was to get myself safely inside the house. The family (not knowing of my transformation) were almost scared out of their senses to see a man tear frantically into the door, with long dishevelled hair streaming over [his] shoulders, and thought me an escaped lunatic. When all was explained, it was very funny to all but Mother, who fears I am losing all the dignity I ever possessed. I know I am getting demoralized, but I should be more so, to mope around and have no fun. During the forenoon one of the men came to the house to get some milk. I told him our cow was gone, that "Jim" had been out hunting her all the morning, and if he thought this demure young lady bore any resemblance to that Jim that he had seen, he did not say, only I imagined he looked

[53]

quizzical, as tho he suspected *something*, and I looked too innocent for anything!

I do not know what this wild life is going to develop in me anyway. Guess I am going to be a "mejium" or spiritualist whether I want to be or not. Father had made me a present of a pair of shell puff combs of which I was very proud. One day the "store boys" and we girls went off on a long tramp hunting plums, perhaps going miles in our wanderings. When I got home in the evening I found I had lost one of my combs, but I knew it would be folly to start out to hunt it after our circuitous wanderings, but I felt so sorry, it worried me half of the night. But I dreamed that I saw my comb on the limb of a certain plum tree I remembered, because it was close to an old deserted cabin a mile from the house. The dream was repeated, and impressed me so queerly, that I was determined to see if there was anything in it, so at daylight I got up quietly and went to the place, led on by an impulse I could not explain. When nearing the spot, and realizing the dreadful stillness and solitude surrounding me, I began to weaken, and think what a fool's errand I was probably bent upon, and altho I almost expected to see a ghost rise up before me, I went to the tree, and there sure enough! just as I had seen it in my dream, *hung my comb!* My hair seemed to rise upon my head and my knees knocked together, but I had my treasure, and had also demonstrated the fact that there *was something* in my dream.

The family were eating breakfast when I got back, bedraggled with dew. Bennet, who is very matter-of-fact, says I must have remembered losing it there, while Mother said, "I did not think you so foolish, Mollie! I thought you were gathering plums." I guess they won't be surprised at *anything* I do these days. They already call me "prophet" and "witch."

Another dream or impression I must tell about. Only

night before last I saw in a dream a closed carriage drive to the door, containing a man and woman, the woman wearing glasses, and a green veil, and the man driving one white and one bay horse. The advent of a female occurs so seldom that we never look for them any more. I announced when I got up that we were going to have company for breakfast and who it would be. I found myself even making some extra preparations. Nothing could seem more improbable at that hour, and the rain pouring down. But Nan, who is a firm believer in my prognostical spasms, was perched by the window to watch the road, and before long an excited exclamation brought us to see the identical carriage, the white and bay horse, the man, and *stranger* yet, the woman with the glasses and green veil. It proved to be one of our Beatrice friends who had gone to the city to meet his wife's sister, a New England schoolmarm. They had tried to reach our place the evening before, but failed, and had to stop at a bachelor's cabin six miles away. The lady was almost eaten up with bedbugs, and declared she would *starve* before eating there, so the brother started at daybreak for our house. When told of my dream, she said she was wishing all night to be with us, and said, "There's no use talking—you are a medium." It's funny anyway, but I cannot explain, nor do I try to.

September 17th

Dora's birthday. Seventeen! I think affairs are coming to a climax between Daily and Dode, and I guess the family will have to acquiesce. They seem happy. He is now batching with Mr. Tucker, who has bought his place, who expects to open up a large farm. I don't know what Mr. Daily's plans are. I hope not to take Dora away. She will be married perhaps before myself, and I, to use a homely phrase, will be left "dancing in the hog trough." Boo! hoo! Boo! hoo!

The second accident that has happened to any of the family occurred a few days ago. The little boys were hunting squirrels. One ran into a hollow log. Sam began chopping to get it out, when Will, who was too impatient to wait, thrust his arm in and down came the ax on his hand, almost cutting it in two, a deep gash across the top that almost scared us to death. Mother fainted, all of the children screamed, and I was the only one that had nerve enough to hold him until Mr. Daily came. He has some knowledge of surgery, dressed and took some stitches in it, but he will carry the scar all his life, and perhaps never go groping into hollow logs again for squirrels.

October 5th

Many days again away from my "Journal."

The golden autumn days have come, and our weather is simply glorious! The leaves are changing from their verdant hues to the yellow and sere, and already they begin to fall, and blighting frosts portend the change of seasons has begun. Soon these leafy spreading branches that have shielded us from summer's suns will be naked and bare, and the bright birds that have cheered us with their melody will seek more genial climes.

Change must come. It is written on everything earthly from the cradle to the grave. It is typical of human life. The Springtime of Youth. The Summer freighted with fruits and blossoms, the Autumn the harvest, and inasmuch as we garner our supplies for winter use, so may we lay up "treasures that will not pass away."

Father has built an addition to the cabin of a neat little frame room, so now we boast of a parlor, or sitting room, and feel that we are getting along wonderfully well. We appreciate every little improvement.

Helena is deserted, Bennet and Favorite leaving soon. One night while they were having a good time, some marauding Indians (it is supposed) walked off with the most of their supplies.

October 15th

We were made glad and happy yesterday by the arrival of our dear grandparents, and sweet cousin Mary. They were hardly expected yet, and no one was in town to meet them, but providence (Grandma says) sent them to Mr. Sanford, who immediately stopped his work and came to pilot them through to this place. The dear old people had made the trip by land from Ind. in their own conveyance, which was an undertaking for a man over 70 years of age. They had made the trip without accident of any kind, until within a few miles of our place the dear old gentleman fell from the wagon and sprained his ankle, and but for By would probably have been killed. So he is a "hero" now with them. Grandma has taken it into her dear old head that he is my lover, and—I guess—well, my Journal, *I* could make a confession here—I believe he is myself. I knew today when he came, and I had not seen him for so long, that I cared a great deal for him. We girls and he sat in the empty covered wagon until midnight last night talking and singing, and some way he found my hand and held it long and tenderly. No one knew it, unless my telltale face has betrayed me today. He has gone away, and a part of me seems to have gone with him. He cannot come as often, as he is busy in town. He can make more by teaming than any other way, sometimes $10 per day.

October 18th [?]

Our cabin was so crowded that Grandfather's have moved into the Hochstetter house. They have taken the land adjoining ours, and will have a house built at once. Then they will be only a few steps from us. It is perfectly wonderful how the old people take matters. They only mourn the absence of church, and already talk of having meetings. We have had a perfect rush for the last few days. There were 22 with our own family to supper last night, several of the Beatrice fellows; they are mostly professional men. I am so busy cooking that I do not get much time to get acquainted. They come around the kitchen tho, in that free and easy way they have out here, and strange to say, I don't care. We are called the Happy Family where there can be something got good to eat, so I am getting up a reputation as a cook. Mr. Pike, one of our guests last night, says I have won the heart of one of the Beatrice widowers (through his stomach, I suppose, as it is said to be the shortest cut).

October 26th [?]

We are having stormy weather again. On Sat. it was threatening a cold storm. Father was worrying about the roof not being done, as he had torn off the clapboards to put on shingles. The children were sick with colds. The urgent necessity of having a good roof above our heads made *me* decide to help Father, and I did too, so it seems I can put my hand to almost anything. We cannot get our new room plastered but have lined it with sheeting and with a good stove it is comfortable.

I do not run thro the woods any more, only occasionally to help the boys gather walnuts and hazel nuts. It is so fortunate that nature has provided so many things here for our use.

I have subsided into a very quiet young lady, with all my native dignity when occasion calls for it, as it did when Mr. Andrew Jackson Cook came to pay his distresses to me the other day. Said he was on the hunt for a wife, and hearing there was a "hull lot of girls" here, he thought he would "come around." I tried to freeze him but don't think I did, as he announced he would come again. I half believe Daily has something to do with his coming (that scamp of a Daily).

November 1st

My Mother's birthday—40 years old. I fear she is a little blue today. I do try so hard to keep cheerful. I don't know as it is hard work to keep myself so, but it is hard with her. She knows now that the children ought to be in school. We will have to do the teaching ourselves.

I did feel discouraged last week when we were all threatened with chills and fever. We had the doctor from Tecumseh, who began dosing the quinine. I took a novel way to cure myself. I went for three successive mornings and jumped into the creek, would then wrap myself in a blanket, rush up to the house, pile into bed and take a sweat. It did cure me too. At least I have no more chills.

By came one day while I was in bed, but only to stay a short time. He bathed my fevered face a little while—perhaps *that* made me better. He cannot come much more this winter. Has sold his mules. Thirty miles is a long way to tramp to see a girl. I'll think of him by day and dream of him by night.

November 10th

I am quite well again, as are all the family. Still plenty of people stopping here. A few days ago the Beatrice widower, Mr. Alexander Mapes, came through, going into Neb. City. He was sick all day here. I dosed him on pepper tea and toned him up with a good supper, which placed him under such great obligations, that he asked me to deal out his rations thro life.

I have had a tender missive from "Andrew Jackson" Cook, asking of me to be a mother to three orphan children. O, which shall I accept? The illustrious "Andrew J." or the brave "Alexander A"?

Mr. Tucker and Holden have gone east for the winter. Holden has built a house and brings his family in the spring. Tucker no doubt goes to get a wife. We do not care for him much.

Grandpa's folks spend their Sundays here. Mary is lovely, but such a delicate girl. Her mother and sister, my dear Aunt Ann and Cousin Amanda, have died with that dread disease consumption, and we fear Mary is not strong. She is improving. Bennet likes her very much. The store boys are going soon, and things *will* be changed when we are alone and travel stops, which will be very soon. Dora and Daily are to be married in May. He goes to N. Y. after Christmas. "Good-by," Mr. Daily.

November 18th

The folks have all been here today. Grandfather will lecture us occasionally, and I know we need it. Perhaps I am too frivolous. I am not as good as I should be, perhaps not as wicked as I *might* be, but I do, I fear, lack in Christian virtues. I say my prayers, and try to practice the golden rule, but I know there is an inward consecration I neglect. I do pray to have revealed to me just *what* I ought to do. I put my shoulder to the wheel, and do what there seems to be required of me, but I am so made up that I must indulge in a "little nonsense now and then," and I hardly think that heaven's door will be closed against me for that.

Father has been building Grandpa's house. Will probably be at home now all the time, as little building is going on in town. He and the boys keep us supplied with wild game. Prairie chickens and squirrels abound here.

Now that Grandfather's are living so near, we are having nice times. Grandma loves to talk about "By," as she already calls him, and I make more of a confidante of her than anyone else. She has a spice of romance in her nature that time nor age can dim.

December 1st

Winter with storms of snow and sleet is here. We live in more or less of a huddle these cold days, but we have enough to eat and plenty of good wood. Father and the boys are cutting and putting up fencing. I write very seldom. The days are short and I don't have much time or quiet. We sew and read, and visit back and forth with Mary and Grandma.

Mr. "A. J." was in a few evenings ago. Daily came in with him, looking too innocent for anything. He got the folks all in the other room to show them something and left us sitting by the kitchen stove. Andrew a-hemmed and a-hawed, thought the "weather was a little warmer than it had been," crossed and recrossed his legs, twirled his thumbs, finally said "he'd been waiting for an answer to his letter." I said, "You are a goose, Mr. Cook, to want a young girl like me. You are old enough to be my father." *Yes*, my grandfather, for all I know! He did not relish this comparison, I imagine, but just then Father came in, and began a conversation, and I slipped out, and up to tell Grandma, who is the recipient of all my woes.

December 17th

My 19th birthday, and O! dear, I feel 25 years if a day. I have grown years, it seems to me, in the last 6 months. I ought to be doing something or making something of myself. There is not much that is flattering in the prospect that looms up before me now; here I am and here I will probably be for some time. I had a nice time thro the summer, but that was a holiday I needed. Now I am ready for something else. Father's burdens are increasing. He needs help, and I shall not mope down here always. By spring I hope something will "turn up" to give me an opportunity to satisfy my ambition.

I sometimes try to picture out my future. Dora's seems settled for her, and everything is lovely. She has such perfect faith in Mr. Daily, but little *we* know what is in store for her. Will I be a happy beloved wife, with good husband, happy home, and small family, or an abused, deserted one, with 8 or 9 small children crying for their daily bread? Or won't I marry at all? If I live to be an *old maid*, I will be one of the good kind that is a friend to everybody and that everyone loves. If I *do* ever marry it will be someone I *love very, very, very* much, better than anyone yet, except—except. Well, if he does love me a *little* he may not think of marriage. I'll wait until he asks *me*.

Christmas, December 25th

I have seen more festive occasions, but after all we were all together, all well, and blest with good appetites. Spent the afternoon in talking over old times with the folks. One can live over again the pleasures of the past. How true that we do not dwell long upon the sad. The day has been clear and not very cold. We took a little walk, just to get the fresh air and aid digestion. No presents were exchanged for the very reason there was nothing to be had. We fixed up the little folks what we could. Poor little tots, they attribute the absence of Santa Claus to not having any chimney. Our stove pipe goes thro a hole in the roof. I wish I might write something nice tonight, but cannot.

New Year's Night, January 1st, 1858

A happy greeting to you, my Journal. Another leaf is turned in life's book, wherein shall be traced the deeds of good or ill. We have our sober reflections on this day, and who is satisfied with the retrospect? There is so much we have done that we should not have done, and so much left undone that should have been done. The past cannot be recalled. We can only drop the tear of penitence over past

misdeeds, and make new resolutions for the future. O!
if we could always keep them, but we are sinful creatures,
poor sinful creatures.

We are invited to spend the day at Mr. Blake's, living 3
miles below us. Mr. Blake was here today. We have not
met his wife, and it was nice for her to ask us. Bennet and
Favorite have been boarding themselves for a while. They
took dinner here today and will go with us tomorrow. By
was to have been here, and I believe his absence has thrown
a little shadow over me. It is so hard to come so far. I ought
not to expect him, I suppose. Now my troubles will begin,
someone to worry over, someone to watch and wait for,
someone to love and weep for.

January 5th

We went to Mrs. Blake's. Mr. Bennet took cousin
Mary, Favorite took Anna, and as a matter of course Daily
took Dora, and *I* was left out in the cold, simply went
along. Mr. Cook came later in the day, and regretted that
he did not know that I had no gallant. (I did not.)

We found Mrs. Blake a lovely little lady, not over 20. A
sweet baby girl has come to bless their home. She gave us
a splendid dinner, and however she got up such a variety
puzzled me, as she cooks by the fireplace and does her
baking in a small covered skillet. The day was so pleasant
we were outside a great deal. We sang and played games
and did not start home until the moon came up. I have
heard of providential interferences, and I hailed Father's
arrival before dark as such, for I should have had to accept
or refuse "Andrew's" escort home. As I started off by
Father's side, the "goose" came up and proffered his arm,
but catching hold of Father's, I said, "How glad I am you
came for me," and the poor fellow had to shank it those
three lonely miles alone. He might have walked along in

our company, but he moped along in the rear. O'er his fate I drop a tear, O, dear. O! dear!

The night was balmy as springtime. The moon shed a soft silvery brightness, lighting up the russet grass until we seemed treading on silver carpets. The young couples ahead enjoyed their walk, but none more than I, with my dear Father, who always enters into my enthusiastic love and admiration of the beautiful in nature.

February 17th

Many weeks have passed since I have written in my "journal." Had neuralgia until my head has been too confused to think. In the meantime affairs have gone on much as usual, with occasionally strangers stopping with us. I have had a beautiful letter from Libbie Scudder. I thought she would forget me, but she seems loyal. She had a long and serious spell of sickness. Her lover was sent for, and *now* she is soon to be married. So she has come off victorious, as I thought. My friend Mollie is engaged, too. O! dear!

By has been to see me again. He looks splendidly, and his visit did me so much good.

One night while here we went up to Grandpa's to spend a while. As we walked along the path admiring the starry heavens, he called my attention to a particular star, and as I turned to look, he kissed me on the cheek! It was *dreadfully* impertinent! and I tried to feel offended. He said "he knew it was wrong and would take it back," but someway, after all, I kept it, to think of, and it burns on my cheek ever since. I like him because he does not flatter, and has a way of looking at me without *saying* silly things. His visit has been like a ray of sunshine in a gloomy prison.

Mr. Daily has gone, and Dora is away off in spirit most of the time. Mary misses Bennet, Anna, Favorite, and such a lot of lovelorn damsels. Cousin Mary is a sort of Madonna style, very quiet and modest. Her father and the rest of the family are coming west.

March 1st

The first of spring has come. It is ushered by terrific winds, but we hail it as the first month of spring. Soon chilling blasts will be succeeded by balmy breezes and pleasant days.

I have a secret, Journal dear. I no longer stand in doubt. I have had a letter, a *sweet* letter, *this* time from a source not to be disregarded. It was not torn to shreds, with a wish that "he would mind his business" as some have been fated, but lies securely next my heart. By loves me tenderly, truly, and has asked my heart in return, and I know now that I can place my hand in his, and go with him thro life, be the path smooth or stormy. I feel like trusting him, more than any lover I ever had. No doubt or misgiving comes into my heart, and I have told him so. We did not fall madly in love as I had always expected to, but have gradually "grown into love." I hope that is an evidence that it will be lasting and eternal. I can endure the lonely hours, for I have someone to dream of and to love, something to look forward to now.

March 20th

Cold and stormy for a week. Nothing of interest has transpired of late. Father has been to "town" and made some purchases and we are busy sewing. I want to help Mother, for as soon as spring opens, I shall go into Neb. City and look about for something to do to help myself. I have never been from home to stay for any time, and would certainly prefer to remain here, but duty and necessity call me elsewhere.

The days are windy and disagreeable. It blows almost continuously.

We have had a couple of days' visit from Mr. and Mrs. Blake, and enjoyed it so much, but I fear we are disenchanted with her husband. When they started home, his horse became balky. Of course it was exasperating, but he treated the poor creature so cruelly, by setting some hay on fire around him, then left him suffering in agony until Father had to shoot him. We were all indignant. Mrs. B. had to come back and stay until he went home and got his oxen. It spoiled all the pleasure we had had, and especially our respect for him. She was very quiet. He has a bad temper and she perhaps understands how to manage him. I am sure I would not know. I *could* not.

April 15th

Since my last writing I have been to Neb. City. Mr. Powel came and took us in his light wagon. They are new neighbors too. He is a "character," and we had a nice trip. The roads were smooth, his horses fresh, and we soon flew over the distance. I visited Mrs. Burnham and Hochstetter, stayed a week, and came home with Mr. George Tucker, who has returned (without a wife. He says he "will marry a Nebraska maiden" yet).

I am to return in a short time to sew for Mrs. Burnham and be with her while her husband goes east for goods.

Now that spring is here I dislike to leave "Hazel Dell," for to me it is the sweetest spot on earth, but I must not be sentimental. I must expect to buffet with the world. I know the path is not strewn with roses to one that has to make their own way, but I have a strong, brave heart, and a faith that teaches me that the Lord will help those that help themselves.

There is a light snowstorm tonight, a little cold again. I hope no hapless wanderer is out on the prairies. We are all at home, seated around our comfortable fireside. I often think of the time when our family circle will be broken, and we seek our homes and fortunes elsewhere. Time is rushing us on to men and womanhood, and soon we will only be children in memory. Already I trace the silver hairs on my Father's brow, and cares are stamping lines on the face of my Mother. May the love and sympathy that has hallowed our home go with us in all after life and, altho our paths may be separate, in heart may we not be divided.

Dora is not well. She has not heard one word from Mr. Daily. He is either dead or unfaithful, and she will not believe him false. The fact of his disposing of his land, and his continued silence, makes *me* think he is not coming back. I have never thought them suited. He is too old, and too exacting for her. She is so trusting, so young, and knows simply nothing of men. She droops and broods over this neglect, and my going from home will throw more care upon her and be a help to employ her mind, and divert her thoughts. Mr. Tucker has no faith in his ever coming back, and really, *I* hope he never will.

CHAPTER FOUR

Nebraska City

May 6, 1858—June 10, 1859

Nebraska City, May 6th

I am now domiciled at Mrs. Burnham's and enjoying my feeling of independence. She is very fond of me and I could not be treated more considerately. She is a woman of the world, however, and very much afraid I may not be taken into society if I am known to be working for her, so she says, "Let them think you are visiting." But no! I said, "My dear, I sail under no false colors. I am henceforth to the public 'Mollie E. Dorsey, dressmaker and seamstress.'" As such I now am, and getting along splendidly. Thanks to a mother's training, I am quite an adept at dressmaking.

Mr. Burnham is away. By spends his evenings with us. Mrs. B. plays the guitar, and we sing a great deal. She is so pleased that By and I are lovers, and makes it very pleasant. Her home is luxurious. She is fond of style and society, while her husband is devoted to business, and, *I* have decided, *entirely uncongenial*. There is a "skeleton" here, I fear. She seems relieved to have him away, has hinted that he was morose and tyrannical, and *so* jealous she is afraid of her life. She is much younger than he, and in her girlhood was a pet and a belle. Too bad they are not suited.

May 15th

A rainy Sunday. I find little time to write in my Journal. Sew all day and spend the evenings with By and Mrs. Burnham. We have frequent visitors beside. Mr. Moore and his son Frank, two southern gentlemen, come in often. The old gentleman comes of afternoons and reads poetry to us, and in the evenings they play cards a while. I still persist in refusing to learn cards. It is hard to get over my early training. By enjoys a game occasionally. Mr. Moore is a widower.

Mrs. Burnham's rooms are in the second story of a large block. They are very pleasant, with low, deep windows where we can sit and view the street below. The lower story is used as headquarters for Majors Russell & Co. freighters.* Today the streets are full of ox teams loading up to start on a trip to Utah. All is commotion, the hallowing of the drivers, the clanking of chains and wagon-masters giving orders. We have noticed a splendid-looking fellow who rides a mouse-colored mule, and who grew more important as he became conscious of our notice. We said, "Now that fellow is too nice looking for that business. He is certainly a professional gentleman, perhaps acting as foreman for pastime. It could not be his occupation." While admiring him today from our porch, I was somewhat disenchanted to hear him *roar* out to one of the men, "Put them thar pans down thar, you gallipin fool, and come *hur*."

---

* Russell, Majors, and Waddell, the largest overland freighting company in operation on the Plains, had selected Nebraska City in 1858 as a staging area and starting point for its wagon trains.

Then someone came up and accosted him with "Hello! Pete," and when "Pete" raised his eyes to gaze at us, somehow the glory had faded, and we found out that he was only plain Peter Byram from Pike Co., Mo. Alas! for the romance! Peter.

June 1st

The weather is lovely and By and I have some delightful strolls of evenings. After I sew all day it is a recreation, and we are becoming better acquainted. *"Little Journal,"* there's no danger of disenchantment there. By is so witty and full of dry fun that he amuses and interests me.

Mr. Burnham has returned, bringing Mrs. Burnham's mother, a lovely old lady.

Pamelia Boulware was buried a few days ago. I think Cornell profited by my advice and suggestions, and brightened her last days by his love and presence. She died in his arms, and I saw him weep over her grave. I wonder if there mingled with his tears some few of repentance, for flirting with me? He pressed my hand at meeting, and no doubt I'll receive another missive. Mr. Burnham is as disagreeable as I had imagined him to be. This morning the biscuit did not suit him, and he "fired" one out at the window. Mrs. B.'s lip quivered and she said, "O! Sam." Another time he pushed over a cup of coffee for the same reason. I don't believe I should be as meek as she, but she says he gives her plenty of money and she does like to dress. She has a carriage and takes me for some pleasant drives. Her little children are very troublesome and quarrelsome and it don't seem much like ours at home.

I wish I were there today beneath the spacious shadow of one of those grand old elms, to have a whiff of the pure air. The hot sun beams down on these brick walls, and not a tree or shrub in the yard.

I am to go home after the "Fourth." Mother objects to my sewing steadily. I am not as well as when out there.

By was in a moment but found me writing. He would "give a penny" to see my Journal, but he won't get the privilege. We are now engaged to be married, but have no definite plans for the future. He has traded for and bought 6 lots south of town, and one lot in Kearney, near the house we first occupied. The value has decreased one-third and he is discouraged about his investment. But as I have said before, I will not marry until I am twenty-one, and by that time, we will be all ready with a home of our own. We will both work for that consummation.

July 5th

Still finds me in Neb. City. I took part in the Fourth of July celebration yesterday at Majors Grove. I sang with the choir. I have made a new acquaintance, a Miss Mollie Eamen. We spent the day together. I attend church regularly, and find some friends among them. Mr. Henry Brown, the gent that helped to move us to the Nemaha, is my class leader and the leader of the choir. He introduced me to a Mr. Harwel today, who made himself very agreeable, and walked home with me. Of course "By" was not in the city. Last week By took me to see some Indiana friends, Mr. and Mrs. Preston. She insists on my visiting her for a while, and as I am thro sewing and cannot go home until an opportunity offers, I will accept the invitation. She has a sweet baby girl, with great blue eyes, and flaxen hair, her mamma's idol is Lily Preston.

July 10th

Am still with Mrs. Burnham for a while. I find it a little dull, as By has been out of the city, but it would be duller but for Mrs. Burnham's love of company, and she is anxious I should have a good time to pay up for my working so hard. I have made the acquaintance of Mr. Peter Byram, and find him, for all his peculiar dialect, a real pleasant fellow.

I am just getting over the effects of having a front tooth gouged out and a new one put in. In an unguarded moment I broke off one that was prepared for filling. The accident happened at dinner one day, and as luck would have it, Mr. Byram sent his compliments, announcing that he was coming in to make his farewell call before going to Utah. *I* was not going to be visible, but Mrs. B. insisted, and said we could fix up a tooth of white wax. It did *look* perfectly natural, and I thought by being careful I could get thro the evening. The time passed pleasantly, so *very* pleasantly that I forgot the existence of my bogus tooth, and when a repartee of "Peter's" called forth a hearty laugh, out came the tooth. I begged to be excused (long enough to replace it, I thought) but lost it entirely, and had no time to make another. I could not go back so disfigured and disenchant the gentleman, so Mrs. B. told him I was sick (of course I was), and with profound regrets at my *sudden* indisposition, he departed, after which we rolled over the floor and laughed until we *were* almost sick, in reality.

I made another tooth the following morning, and while standing on the balcony looking down on the street, Mr. Byram looked up and spoke, and as I opened my mouth to reply, *out* came the treacherous tooth again and took him on the head. I drew back and stepped inside, when he came puffing up the steps to see what I was offended at, and there was nothing to do but make a clean breast of it. He thought it improved my looks, I was so rosy and blushing, and "my image should go with him, on his dreary journey across the plains, if I did not have a tooth in my head." After which he bade me good-by, and I wished him a safe journey and we parted. Father came in town that day and took me to the dentist, and I won't have to resort to wax substitutes any more.

July 15th

I am visiting Mrs. Preston. Attended the sewing society and supper at Mrs. Hamlin's. Mr. Harwel, the gentleman I met on the "Fourth," is their guest, and he was devoted, all the evening. It is a lonely walk to Mrs. Preston's, and I accepted his escort home, and also to and from church next Sunday evening. By and I have been so seldom in public that our engagement is not generally known nor credited, and he told me when he went away to not go out of nights alone. I love to go to church and he does not, and Mrs. Preston says, "Go with someone long enough to bring him to a sense of his indifference in that respect." Mrs. P. is a real goose about me anyway. She will fix and fuss with my dress when I go out, has a great many little ornaments with which she likes to adorn me, "just to make me look sweet," and if [I] am *more* attractive for that, *she* is to blame. It is nice to have someone so motherly, and I try to repay her by helping generally. She is Mr. Preston's opposite entirely. He is younger than she, and her second husband. By says she has a history, so she wears the halo of a heroine to me.

Monday, July 20th

I have just a whole lot to tell you, little book. Well, Mr. Harwel came early and spent a couple of hours with Mrs. P. and I, then we went to church, and perhaps if it had not have been a soft moonlight night he would not have tried to talk sentimental, but he did, and it has bothered me considerably, for I don't want to listen to such stuff. However, he went on to say, with little of the preliminary, that he was very much interested in me, that I was the counterpart of an angel girl whom he was engaged to marry but she died. He had been told that I would never marry Mr. Sanford, and that if I would accept him we would go to Europe! that he was rich, and I should never want for anything.

Mrs. Hamlin says he has more money than he knows what to do with, and that I should look out for money as well as love, that By is *good* but not rich! Yes, I said, and he is so *very, very* good that I should take him, and Mr. Harwel is dispossessed of the idea that he is nothing to me, but after all I have promised to ride into the country with him tomorrow.

July 21st

Mr. Harwel called to take me riding. I ought not to have gone, I suppose, but it was *such* a temptation to ride, and get a whiff of fresh air, and I knew I could take care of myself.

I did enjoy the ride. We had a long talk. He is not young nor handsome, but intelligent and religious. He seemed so honest and earnest, and I did not defraud my darling when I gave him kind words, and promised to remember him sometimes in my prayers. I told him frankly of my engagement, and Mrs. Hamlin is to blame for encouraging him. So we said good-by, and he leaves for his home tomorrow. By came a few moments after I got home. I have told him all about it, and it is all right.

Well, I am going home in a day or two, to settle down again, and will probably have no more experiences. I am real homesick anyway. The folks are working hard trying to farm, Mother and the girls raising chickens, and enjoying life very well. Dora is not well—she is grieving for that scamp, Daily, who has never written her a word nor have we heard anything direct about him, and I'm not much surprised.

August 4th

Home again from the city to the sweet quiet of "Hazel Dell."

Everything looks so fresh and lovely. The woods seem greener and the flowers brighter than *ever* before. Mother is overworked, and as I have done no hard work I can go at it again with a relish. I have been away three months, three whole months!

Cousin Mary's father, our Uncle Henry, has come with the remnant of his family to live in Neb. He will go to Neb. City and Mary will go to be his housekeeper. It will be nicer for Mary. Her life is too prosy at Grandfather's. The old people are happy now that they have church services at the old store building on the Hill. R'vnd John Chivington * often preaches for them.

I believe Cousin Mary liked Mr. Bennet more than is good for her peace of mind. No one will know it, though. She will only be more quiet and live more within herself.

August 10th

The whole family, Mother and we children, went off on a picnic yesterday, or rather to hunt patches of elder-berries and grapes. The larger boys took the smaller ones in a cart, and we just scoured the country. We whooped and hurrahed until we were hoarse, just because we thought no one lived near to hear us, and to hear the echoes as they rang thro the woods. We travelled about four miles. We were mistaken, however, about no one being around, for

* Reverend John M. Chivington, a Methodist minister, came to Nebraska in 1856. In 1860 he went to Colorado as presiding elder of the Rocky Mountain District. At the outbreak of the Civil War he was chosen as major of the First Colorado Volunteer Regiment and saw service against Confederate forces in New Mexico. In November 1864 he led the Third Colorado Cavalry against Black Kettle's band of Cheyenne and Arapaho in the controversial action at Sand Creek, Colorado.

in the afternoon we saw a horseman coming to where we had stopped to rest. He was quite excited. His wife had sent him out to hunt the Indians that she was *sure* was on the warpath. He was as much surprised as we, but invited us to go over to their cabin. They were an old couple without a family, and had only just come to the place, and did not know of our existence. We stayed a while and the good old gentleman took we women folks home with his team..

People are settling all around us, and Sundays there is quite a congregation at the "church." One day Dora went off into the woods by herself. Poor dear, she is pining for her truant lover. When she came in her face was perfectly radiant. She told me she had been praying, and had felt herself converted, and I believe she is. She is goodness itself, anyhow, but her face wears another look. Surely His grace is sufficient for us. Surely a conversion like that must be real, since there has been no exciting meeting nor anything, but the convictions of her own heart. God keep my good sister.

How well I remember when *I* felt *my* sins forgiven. O! why am I not always good? I am afraid I am too frivolous, that is, to do other people much good. Grandpa lectures me constantly. His piety is of the severe type, where it is almost a sin to laugh. Poor dear old gentleman thinks it is an unpardonable sin for us to wear hoops, but we think to be out of the world and out of fashion too is a little too hard, so we persist in the style, and when the boughten ones give out, we substitute small grapevines. He said one day, "Mary (he always calls me M-a-r-y), you cannot hope to enter heaven with those hoops." "No. No, Grandpa, nor will *you* with your long tailed coat." No, Grandpa, we will wear robes, and heaven grant *I* may deserve one. I am sorry to see my good sister Dora so unhappy. She knows we do not like Mr. Daily, so she is quiet, and we respect her sorrow, but all think she will get over her disappointment.

September 1st

Where have I been? Well, I've been at work gathering and putting up fruit, and regaining the color and strength I had lost while in the "city."

Mr. Tucker has been boarding here almost all summer. He has had a spell of chills and fever, and I have been his nurse. In fact, no one could manage him in his delirium but me. When he had his spells of raving, they would all leave the room, but I could lay my hand on his head, and he would quiet down. We are good friends.

By has been out for a whole week, helping Father cut his hay. Of course *I* enjoyed it, and coming at a time of need, Father will appreciate it all the more. We have loads of fine vegetables and revel in watermelons. Father's grain will not amount to much, as it has been too dry and did not fill out well.

September 15th

Yesterday we went up to see our neighbors, the Powels, and Townsends—two families that have settled on the creek above us. The Powels are Missouri people. Mrs. P. did not evidently appreciate the trouble we had taken to call upon her. Said she "had no time for 'fooling' " and spent the most of her time chasing the hens in the barnyard and "whaling" the youngsters with which they are numerously blest. I went out once to look around, and found her behind the cabin smoking her pipe, a huge corncob. This was perhaps to settle her nerves, for before a great while we were invited out to dinner, a nice one, too. When I offered to help with the dishes, she looked surprised. "Pap had told her we were sort of stuck up and *I* stayed in town a heap" and she "*never* did like town folks," but I believe I *mollified* her considerably by amusing the children and helping her, so that when we left she insisted on my coming back.

We went to Townsends for supper. We only intended calling at both places, but could it would not do not to eat with them. We *must* stay. Mr. Tucker, who had taken us, was willing, so after all we had a pleasant day. The Townsends have a lot of half-grown boys. Mr. Townsend was very jolly. Said he had been trying to get his boys to "come a-courtin'." The young cubs put on sagacious looks, and about next Sunday they will be here in force. Nan insisted on their coming, and she will have to dispose of them, but she is equal to *this* emergency.

We called at Mr. Holden's, who have only lately arrived. The family consists of his wife, two young sons, and Miss Wilson, a maiden sister of Mrs. Holden. They are lonely enough, and wish themselves back in N. Y. I told Mr. Tucker as long as he had decided to marry in this country here was his chance for Miss Wilson had remarked that she "didn't suppose girls ever would have a chance to marry out here." Mr. Tucker proposes to make his own selection. They are to spend the day with us this week, and we must try to be neighborly, and have Mr. Tucker as guest.

Sunday, September 20th

Just as I thought, the whole Townsend family have been here to spend the day. The boys scarcely left their father's side. He does the talking for the whole family. The boys would give out a loud guffaw! or a silly snicker at every remark. Finding it impossible to entertain the trio of boys, we devoted ourselves to the old gent. We won't *insist* on their coming again and Nan has her dose for once!

I have had a sick spell. Been in the hot sun too much, and perhaps ate too much wild fruit. I have spent 3 days in bed, and am quite weak. The weather is fine. Services were held today at Grandpa's house by R'vnd Chivington. He took dinner with us.

October 5th

Our weather is delightful, almost like summer. I do not work much. Am playing the "role" of invalid quite gracefully, so I wander around the woods, and spend many hours with my precious Grandma, who pets and loves me continually, the darling.

Today I took my old composition book and went off over the creek by the new haystack to be alone and un-molested. Everything had a tendency to make me feel senti-mental. I laid me down by the fragrant hay, and looking up through the crimson and golden foliage of the grand forest trees, I could see patches of the blue sky, and watch the feathery clouds drift and float away, until they seemed throngs of white-robed angels soaring up into the golden portals of heaven. Bright birds twittered above me. Anon the echo of a song came floating across from the home and sounds of gleeful sports from the little children reached my ear. I was wooed into a slumber and awoke refreshed. In reviewing some of my old manuscript, I came across a little piece I wrote at school about a dying girl. I wished that I might convert it into verse. The sentiment was in my heart and the jingle of rhyme in my head, and, invoking my Muse, I soon scribbled some lines which I copy in my Journal.

The Dying Girl's Dream

'Twas a gentle summer's evening.
  Blue and golden was the sky.
In a widow's lowly cottage
  A young girl laid to die.
Slowly gathered death's dark shadows

O'er her pale but heaven lit face
Where it seemed no earthly sorrow
E're had found a resting place.

Calmly there a mother kneeling
    Prayed for strength in that dark hour.
Angels whispered, "Meek submission.
    God has sent us for your flower.
We will bear her where no sorrow
    Ere shall cloud her happy face.
Would you keep her from that heaven
    In this cold and cheerless place?"

* * * *

"Mother dear, I *see* an angel!
    'Tis the same I saw last night.
I am passing thro the river,
    But ahead I see the light.
Fare thee well, my darling Mother.
    On the shores the angels stand,
Swelling loud the mighty chorus,
    Welcome to the 'Better Land.' "

When the midnight's gentle moonbeams
    Fell across that cottage floor,
She had joined those waiting angels
    Reached that river's golden shore.
Thus may we, when angels summon
    Us, from off this mortal strand,
Find a safe and welcome entrance
    Into heaven's Better Land.

I have many seasons of sublime and poetic thoughts, and often soar above the cares of life into a world of my own, into whose portals no one may invade.

It is well perhaps that I have to battle with stern realities.

I might become an idle dreamer, for I have not talent enough to make much of myself. I used to dream of being an author, of climbing the steeps of fame, but *Fate* has led me from the realms of Poesy and Thought into a sea of perplexities and cares. I have faith though that my life's work will be appointed, that my heavenly Father will show me my duties and my way. Out in the broad harvest fields of life there is work among the laborers. There I can lend a helping hand, there give a word of comfort, here a word of cheer, and if I can be up and doing, it were better than to devote my time and energies to dreaming and rhymes. By is a good match for me. He is so thoroughly matter-of-fact and practical that it will help equalize my romance and sentiment. He often brings me from my airy flights. He is good and sensible and, bless his heart, *I love him*.

Our associations here are not congenial, the people rough and ignorant. I suppose I ought to go to work and do something to help and elevate them. But where shall I begin? Of course there is room for self-improvement, and as "charity begins at home," I need not look outside for a subject, for goodness knows I need it.

November 1st

Mother's birthday again. It does not seem a year since I chronicled the last one. Time flies, its speed we cannot stay. Mother's health is better, and I do not see that she looks as old quite, as she did a year ago.

Well, my "Little Journal," I've something to tell today. Mr. Daily has come back. We had heard a few days ago that he was at St. Joseph, Mo., and had talked over the event of his coming. We almost feared he might, and would try to excuse his actions, and that Dode might forgive and take him back.

One day last week he knocked at the door, and walked in

as if he had only been gone a day. He had the cheek to be as profuse in his greetings as tho everything was right.

They had an interview, and he gave as his reason of silence and absence that he had seen so many unfaithful women, and had determined to test her love, altho he insisted that he had written. But we *know* that he had not.

She finally told him absence had conquered all she had ever had for him, and they parted, and Dora is more like her old self again than she has been since he first went away.

I am to leave home again. Mrs. Bond, who lives 8 miles away, has come for me to sew for her. I don't want to go. Mr. George Gedney, her young brother, says he will bring me home every Sunday. Only too happy to get the chance.

December 20th

I have been at Mrs. Bond's several weeks. I have no chance to get lonely, as I have been busy and the family is large.

"George" reads to us of evenings. He is inclined to be sentimental.

By is now clerking in Mr. Bond's store at Neb. City. Mr. Bond comes home once a week and I always get a letter. I was over home on my 19th [20th] birthday, the 17th. I tried to get George interested in some of the girls, but he acts a little soft with me just because there are no other girls around. I shall have to put a stop to his reading love stories and poetry. They are too suggestive. The hired girl makes herself especially attractive and is a far prettier girl than I. He does not like By, and "By" does not *dote* on him particularly.

January 1, 1859

Another new year. I wonder if I am any better than I was one year ago. I ought to *know* more, but I don't know as I do. I find by reviewing some of these pages that I still say silly things, and sometimes make unfavorable comments about people and things, but after all, the little talks we have, my "little book," are confidential. They are not gossip. We are all jogging along in the even tenor of our way, about as we did last winter. There has been very heavy snows, and terrible high water, the whole country flooded.

By came with a carriage and brought me home from Mrs. Bond's. We had to go miles out of our way to find a safe crossing of the Nemaha, so it took us almost all day to get home, but we had a nice visit, and considered it no great calamity. I was so glad to get home. It does not seem to me that I can ever leave home entirely. Few girls love their home and family any better than I.

"Be it ever so humble there's no place like home." But when spring comes again I will be off to Neb. City to help myself. Cousin Mary's father has married, very suddenly too. He has been here so short a time. The girls are very unhappy with their stepmother, and By says that they will have trouble.

Holdens and Blakes visit us frequently, but new roads being laid out thro the country, we do not have as much travel. We are all well, content, and happy. Mr. Tucker is in Chicago again. Miss Wilson has *soured* on him since he woos no more.

February 15th

My little book, I had my "valentine" from By and two or three from other sources. Sometimes I wish By was a little more demonstrative, a trifle more sentimental. He is very matter-of-fact, and yet I presume if he were, I would soon tire of him. *I know* that he loves me, and that is enough for a sensible girl.

[83]

February 28th

For a week we had very cold, disagreeable weather. It was a little dull. I feel sad and depressed today from the effects of one of my *dreams* last night. All the night long when I slept I could see my Cousin Mary first a bride and then in her coffin, and waking, I seemed to hear her calling me. Mother says I am *morbid* and must have a change, but no! there's something wrong and I fully expect before night to hear bad news. I find myself looking toward the hill where we first get a sight of teams. I wish I were not this way and maybe after all I am *morbid* or something else. I do not dwell on imaginary or impending evils, and these impressions come unsolicited. I hope I'll throw it off, for in this world of mishap and troubles, if we always knew of them beforehand we could not be very happy. All of the spirit promptings I want is to be good and true.

Neb. City, March 5th

At Mrs. Preston's. I have been in town a week. My "dream" did portend trouble, sure enough. The night of the day I last wrote here, about dusk, Uncle Frank Dorsey rode up to the door on horseback. The moment I saw him my heart beat faster. I said, "Uncle, you bring bad tidings." He looked surprised and said, "Who told you?" I said, "What is it?" He said, "Your Cousin Mary has had a hemorrhage and cannot live, and is constantly calling you." We sent for Mr. Tucker, who has recently returned, and he kindly offered to take me in town. So early next morning we came, and found the dear girl a trifle better, but the doctors say she cannot live. I have been with her constantly, until today I came to Mrs. Preston's, where I am to make my home, by her kind invitation, whenever I am in town.

I do not like the stepmother. She has a natural antipathy

to Mary, but treats Anna, the younger sister, better. Mary is so angelic and patient, too much of a saint for *her*.

As I sat by the cradle of little Lily today, we were mutually admiring her baby loveliness. Some thoughts occurred to me. I will write them here. Her Mamma said, "O! Mollie, you have expressed my thoughts exactly." As I read, she pressed her to her heart.

> Little Lily—gentle Lily
> Smiling in her cradle laid
> While a Mother sweetly wondered
> If so bright a gem could fade.
>
> * * * * *
>
> Eyes that sparkle from their blue depths
> FIlled with innocence and glee;
> How the little tongue will prattle
> When I hold her on my knee.
>
> * * * * *
>
> Heaven grant to keep our Lily
> Pure and beautiful as now
> That no heavy clouds of sorrow
> Ere may shade her happy brow.

By is not in the city, is now at a small town invoicing goods and helping settle up some business. I have only seen him once. He is looking well. We will not be married this spring. Some of the friends shake their heads and say, "Long engagements are not good," but we understand the situation, and I suppose we are the parties most interested. It strikes me people worry themselves too much over it.

March 10th

Have been nursing Mary for another week, and very tired. It was made more difficult by the stepmother's dislike of me. How my Uncle could have married a woman of her type to succeed my pure sweet Aunt I cannot divine. She seems to have a power over him, and Mary feels she is neglected by her father. She knows she cannot live and talks sweetly about going to meet the loved ones. She wants me to be with her at the last. I would not leave her at all if I could stand the wear and tear.

I have made the acquaintance of a Mrs. Arnold, widow, who teaches in the city schools. She has interested herself in my behalf, and secured me a position in a school north of town. I begin the first of April, "all fools day." Hope there's nothing prophetic in that.

Mrs. Burnham has moved from her home in the block to other quarters, and I seldom see her. Her husband and By have had some little business troubles, and I fear we are hardly as good friends as we formerly were.

I have handed my church letter into the M. E. church and will take a class in S. S. I am to board around among the scholars, and spend my Sundays at Mrs. Preston's, as it will be too far to attend church. It is fully two miles from here. I don't know how I shall like teaching, but Mrs. Arnold thinks I will make a success of it. I am not as robust as I was two years ago.

March 15th

I seldom write now, I spend so many nights by Mary's side. The distance from Mrs. Preston's is one and a half miles up there, and up hill all the way, and these windy days make the walk very hard. Going up the other day, I found a few violets, and carried them to her. She laid them on the pillow by her face. As they drooped and wilted she said, "O! Mollie, I shall be soon where flowers never die," and she will be all too soon, for she is failing rapidly. Her disease is quick consumption.

The stepmother has ordered me to stay away, but I shall

not do it. She dislikes me, I think, because they all like me better than they do her. She wants to be first and foremost.

April 15th

I have found little time to write since I assumed my new duties. I opened my school on the day appointed. I have 20 scholars, mostly young children. It is a kind of Mormon settlement and I don't like it much. I stood the "boarding around" just two weeks, and today have moved into permanent quarters. The first place was with a southern family. Their manner of living is so different from ours that it just about used me up. For breakfast we had corn bread, salt pork, and black coffee. For dinner, greens, wild ones at that, boiled pork, and cold corn bread, washed down with "beverage." For supper we had hoe cake, cold greens, and pork with coffee. The "beverage" was put upon the table in a wooden pail and dished out in tin cups. When asked if I would have some of the "aforesaid," I said "yes," thinking it perhaps was cider, but found out it was vinegar and brown sugar and warm creek water.

At this place I slept upon the floor, and festive bedbugs held high carnival over my weary frame the night through.

The next week was with a rather nice family who lived nicely, but my digestive organs were in such a state I could not eat. When I found out I had to either go back to "beverage" and greens, or into a Mormon family with four children and two small rooms, I utterly refused to teach. Mr. Cole, one of the directors, came to the rescue and brought me to his house, where I have a nice room and everything comfortable. The first thing I should do is to offer up thanks for my deliverance, and *diet* myself until I can eat my accustomed rations. I have been warned that I won't stay here long, as Mrs. Cole is a "termagent" and "jealous of every woman that comes around." I don't worry over that, for I have some faith in my knowledge of people and things, and being forewarned is forearmed.

April 25th

I am getting along quite well with my school, altho these days are depressing. The leaves are putting forth, and spring is again with us. My children range from six to nine years, and of course the younger ones are restless! but I have won their love. My schoolhouse stands in a pretty grove, and wild flowers are so abundant the schoolroom is a perfect bower.

Better than all, I have established myself with Mrs. Cole. I could see at first that she was not very well pleased. I did not blame her much, as her boarder brought no financial benefit, as they had no children as scholars. Being on a farm, she had a great deal of work, so the first Saturday I was there I went into the kitchen to do some work for *my*self, and offered to assist her. At first she was so stiff and unfriendly, but when I told her I was a "country girl" and could do lots of things and loved to work, we were soon on quite friendly terms. After dinner she *insisted* on Mr. Cole taking me to town in the carriage.

I do quite a little for her, and she said today she was glad to see me come home, I made a little life. Her maiden sister I thought one of the sourest persons I ever met, but she is real pleasant, and I can get them all into a good humor by recounting some of our exploits on the farm. *Bless* the old sweet "Hazel Dell." I get frequent letters and get homesick too, but three months will soon have passed away.

I spent last Sunday with Mary. She will only last a few days, and they have promised to send for me when the end approaches. By was down to see me on Sat. evening. We regret we cannot meet more often, but such is fate.

May 4th

I come with saddened heart and tearful eyes today, my Journal. This afternoon Mary was laid away. She called for me the eve before she passed away. Through the stepmother's misrepresentations I did not get the message, and only heard of the event in time to reach the house for the funeral services. Everyone was wondering at my absence. She remarked that I had shown my affection, that she had sent a messenger direct to me. Of course she did *not* do it. When I entered the room, she rushed up and threw her arms about me, saying, "Our darling is gone. O! why did you not come?"

There was no time for exposing her deception, and I only had a moment to look my last on the dear sweet face. By was there and walked home with me to Mrs. Preston's. Poor little Anna, she is left alone, and seems so bereft. There are two brothers, John and Wymond. They were once a large and happy family but O! how changed! My Aunt was my mother's only sister. I promised Mary to write some verses about her when she was gone, and have paid a small tribute to her memory.

May 15th

The days are lovely. Spring has opened earlier than usual, I think.

I was thinking the other day how nicely and smoothly I was getting along. Not an unpleasant event had occurred at school nor at home. But a day or two ago I had to inflict my first corporal punishment. After exhausting my powers of moral suasion with little Johnnie Morton, to establish my authority and make an example, I chastised him, very mildly.

He did not come back to school the next day, nor the next, and hearing he was sick, I went over last evening to see him. They are very poor people living in a shanty in the woods. The mother met me very nicely, and Johnnie was pleased to see me. He had chills and fever. The mother said the boys had told of the punishment, and, Johnnie being taken sick the next day, the grandmother, who is over 80 years of age, imagined he had been injured. The mother told me not to mind anything the old lady said, as she was childish, and he being her pet, she would not allow *them* to punish, if she could help it. Very soon the old lady came hobbling into the room, and when she found out I was the "teacher," she began a perfect torrent of abuse, and but for her age and infirmity I could not have stood it. I said, "Why! Grandma, Johnnie was not hurt. Were there any marks on his body?" "No, but he's hurt 'inside eternally.' " (I suppose she meant *internally*.) "Yes," she shrieked, "and *you* a *church member*. Well! if *you* go to heaven, *I* don't want to go." I don't know but that she would have struck me with her crutch she was so irate, but the son came in and led her out of the room. He then came back and said "it was all right, that Johnnie should come to school again when he got well," but the whole thing was so unexpected and undeserved that I came home and cried myself to sleep.

Today there was the queerest little Frenchman * came to the schoolroom door and handed me a bouquet of lovely flowers. He could not express himself very plainly, but it sounded like, "Ze young ladee, she look like ze flower," and with the flourishes and smiles and bows, I considered it the greatest compliment I ever had. I find he is employed at Mr. Draper's floral gardens, not far from here. I have

* The "Little Frenchman" was Hippolyte Giradot who had come from France to Nebraska City with his father, who died within a few weeks after his arrival. The young man was taken into the home of Joel Draper, a nurseryman. In 1861 Giradot went to Colorado as a freighter where he again met Mollie (see p 159). He married a niece of Draper and settled in Orchard, Colorado, where he died in 1922.

seen him pass often and he always bows and smiles, and I bow and smile. During my leisure moments mornings and evenings I have been making Mrs. Cole a dress. She is so pleased with it, and we get along splendidly. Someone said before I came that if I ever talked to Mr. Cole she would pull my hair out by the roots, but I nearly talk him blind as I do everyone else, and have lost none of my raven tresses yet. I meet By at Mrs. Preston's almost every Sunday. He is looking splendidly and *I love him more and more.*

June 10th

    I am not at all well. The hot weather and teaching does not agree with me but my school closes very soon, by the last of the month. I will have taught 4 months instead of the three. Johnnie came back and I have had no further hostilities.

    Father was in to see me. He says I look drooping, and I must come home. He does not want to see my color go. There is nothing like the atmosphere of "Hazel Dell" to restore that, and I can scarcely wait to see the dear ones there. Father has rather better luck farming this year, altho he does not confine himself to that, but works alternately in town.

    I was very much surprised yesterday as I was about to leave the schoolroom after dismissing the little ones. I noticed a gentleman hitching a mouse-colored mule to the post, and directly, who should come up to the door but Mr. Peter Byram himself, bronzed and tanned but handsome as ever. We had a laugh over the tooth scrape, and he admitted that I did look better since the dentist had furnished a genuine one. I was still further surprised when he made known the object of his visit. He came to propose marriage. "He did not believe I was going to marry Mr. Sanford or I wouldn't be teaching school." Beside, he had heard that he had left the country. Whether he storied or someone told him for sport I do not know. I only know he's a goose.

I did not accept Mr. Byram. He told me of his possessions, and position with the Company as much as to say, "All shall be thine if thou wilt marry me." I asked Peter if he would have a girl that would throw off an honest man if he was poor, to marry for money. He said he would marry *me* under any circumstances. Assuming all the dignity and indignation I could command, I said, "Mr. Byram, you have insulted me. I bid you good day." With queenly tread and flushing cheek, I wended my homeward way, leaving him to untie his mule and gallop off his chagrin. This morning I had a note, begging me to consider him a friend and a gentleman, and wishing me eternal happiness with Mr. Sanford.

I am at Mrs. Preston's to spend Saturday and Sunday as usual. The Coles bring me over in the carriage. By and I took a ramble over on the hill south of town where he has 6 lots. It is a high bluff overlooking the river, with a grove of fine old walnut trees. We sat there in the cool evening shade, and had a lovely visit, talked over our affairs. Some day we may have a home up here. Times are so dull there is nothing to be done at By's trade, blacksmithing and carriage-making. I do not like the business anyhow, and want him to go at something else. Mr. Byram whirled by us in his buggy as we were wending our steps homeward. He bowed and looked wistfully back, and By had to listen to another of my confessions. Bless him, he is not jealous, for he knows I am truly his sweetheart, and his alone, *alone*.

CHAPTER FIVE

Hazel Dell and Nebraska City

July 4, 1859—April 8, 1860

July 4th

At home again. By brought me out in a carriage, and we had a lovely ride. I find all well and so happy to see me. The little brothers cling to me with affectionate tenderness. I have many little stories to tell them of my schoolchildren. I could take the school this fall again, but it is not a paying affair. The people are too poor. Beside, Father says I cannot teach again. It is too trying on me. I am working in my old harness again, and enjoy it. I am only too happy to lighten Mother's burdens. The home looks clean and comfortable. Sweet "Hazel Dell," how happy I am to be once more within your charming precincts.

We had no particular demonstrations today, only the good dinner we generally get up for the children. By went home the next day after he brought me out. Livery bills are too high to linger long away, and times too hard to be idle.

We have frequent calls from the neighbors. The Holdens

[93]

and our folks are quite intimate. Mr. Daily is stopping with Tucker a while, and, strange to say, called with him to see *me*, they said. I suppose that was to take off some of the cheekiness of Daily's coming. I cannot understand that man anyhow, and anyone would suppose he would not come again. Dora merely noticed him.

She is looking well and happy again, and his appearance did not affect her equilibrium in the least.

Grandpa has the P. O. now, so that we see all of the people around here quite often. Cousin Anna has been out on a visit since Mary died. I think Uncle will separate from his wife. I have only been there a few times. She pretends to have gotten over her dislike of me. But I dare not trust her.

July 20th

The days are passing pleasantly, only it is suffocatingly hot. We are taking life as easily as possible. We thought it the right thing to return some of the visits of our neighbors. We do not go a great deal on account of having nothing but oxen to drive, unless we walk, which Mother cannot do.

A carriage had been left here for a while, and by dint of persuasion and promises to be extra careful, Grandpa let us take "Bonny," his pet mare, and Mother, the little boys, and I started to see the Townsends. We had a fine ride of two miles. Came to the creek, where the bridge did not look too safe, but I thought by walking and leading the horse I could cross safely. But just as she took the last step, her hind legs went through a hole, and then she began floundering and kicking until I supposed she would kill herself. I soon had Mother and the boys out of the carriage and then started for help. In the field a half mile away were some men harvesting By perching myself on the rail fence, screeching until I was hoarse, and frantically waving my shawl, I attracted their attention. They soon came to the rescue. The poor horse had tried to extricate itself, until perfectly exhausted, but when set free, had no broken bones, but was dreadfully barked up, and then like a goose, or rather a woman, I sat down on the ground and cried.

We made our visit, however, and came home in the evening late. We met Grandpa on the road. We took him in to ride, and but for a slight limp the horse went as lively as ever, and, strange to say, the old gentleman did not scold, but I think we will make our other calls in the ox team with Sam or Will to drive for us, or else we will stay at home.

August 5th

By has been out again, *this* time to say good-by. He has had some word from his old stepfather and thinks he ought to go and see him before he dies, and altho I can hardly bear to see him go, I do not want to keep him from any duty he owes to his father. But I do feel that if he goes I shall never see him again. No lack of faith in him, but a fatality that would follow. He only stayed two days this time.

When he started to go back to town I walked over through the woods with him. He had forgotten his gloves, and had to go back to the house. While he was gone I wrote a few lines in his memorandum book I had borrowed.

When he came back and found me crying, he said he had a notion not to go, and then I felt ashamed of my selfishness. We lingered as long as possible, and I watched him out of sight in defiance of the old adage that it was a "bad sign," all the time in my heart saying:

> The time has come for us to part,
> To speak the last farewell,
> And sorrow casts upon my heart
> Her sad and weary spell.

I fain would send you on your way
With parting words of cheer,
But sobs will choke their utterance
While your loved form is near.

*   *   *   *   *

But I will live upon the past
O'er each bright happy day.
Their memory will warm my heart
When *you* are far away.

And when I lay me down to sleep
After the day is done,
I'll pray that heaven may vigils keep
Over the absent one.

But should stern fate our paths divide,
By fate our hearts be riven,
We'll meet up on that other side—
We'll be as *one* in heaven.

I do not want to be mawkish or *too* sentimental, but I cannot help my natural feelings.

But this shadow will soon pass, and I must not forget that I cannot *entirely* control my own destiny. I am naturally hopeful. To be sure I have my moments of misgivings. Flitting shadows sometimes cross my pathway, but thanks to a kind Providence I have never yet had real cause for sorrow, but my life is not lived out yet. Happily for us, the future is hidden from our view. Sorrow may be in store for me.

August 10th

My "darling's" birthday. Have had a letter. His trip is now postponed until later. Could those pathetic lines have changed his mind?

Are the ties of love stronger than those of kinship? He

said he read the "lines" as he trudged over the prairie, and made up his mind he would not leave me if he could possibly avoid it.

I have also had a letter from Mrs. Bond, who has engaged me to sew for 6 weeks. She has moved to Neb. City and wants the children fixed for school. So by the first of September I am off from home again.

August 20th

Mother and I have made several other visits. Dora went with us to Mr. Holden's. There we met Daily. Wonder if he is shining around Miss Wilson? She is a better match than Dora would have been. Mr. Holden is a genuine spiritualist, but the family are not, so I judge there is no very close "affinity" between them. They are genuine New England people, lovely housekeepers and good cooks. I am busy helping Mother put up the early fruit. The wild plums are good this year. We do not have much travel now, so our housework is lighter. The girls have taken my place somewhat, since I have been from home so much. I am feeling better, and ready to start to work again. I have been offered the school, but declined. I believe I prefer sewing, unless I could be a first-class teacher.

August 25

Mr. Tucker kindly brought me into town. I am with Mrs. Preston for a few days. She claims me when not otherwise engaged. I find her very unwell, and so despondent. They are not very prosperous, and it seems to worry her. I frequently find her crying. I wrote some verses for her today hoping they might help brighten her skies.

Little "Lily" grows more beautiful every day. Her mother idolizes her.

August 28th

I walked up on the hill to see Cousin Anna, and look at Mary's grave. She requested to be buried in the front dooryard. Anna is desolate without her sister. The stepmother was too sweet for anything, but back beneath those glittering eyes I can see something I would not trust.

September 10th

Am duly installed at Mrs. Bond's. George is still dancing attendance, and every wish I express is more than gratified. He *is* a nice boy. I attended a church supper at the Hamlin House last night. Met many pleasant friends. Mrs. Hamlin says Mr. Harwel always inquires about me. I get scarcely no time to write. By comes around of evenings and we walk, and enjoy each other's society.

Mr. Bond is in the south, and she and I are alone later of evenings, and have a great deal to talk over, mostly to keep her from being lonely. She seems to adore her husband. Her children are pretty and very well behaved. I spend my Sundays as usual at Mrs. Preston's. She is feeling better. I was surprised the other day to see the verses I wrote for Mrs. Preston in the weekly paper. She had sent them up, and had them published, to preserve them for herself, she says. The Editor is a mutual friend, and has solicited contributions, but mercy! I never dreamed of having that jingle published. Mr. Harvey says I have the talent, and not to "bury it under a bushel," but I am sure I shall never pose as an author or writer. But I do often wish that I might be something more than a mere machine. There is something dull in sitting here day by day, planning this garment and making that, but it seems to be my destiny just now. There does not seem to be much that a girl *can* do here. O! well, I ought to be satisfied that I can do as much as I do, for it is a great help to the family.

Mrs. Burnham called today, and she, By, and I took a stroll up to the lots. I had not seen her for a long time. She looks troubled and worn. Reverses have come to them, and I fear she is not the one to meet them bravely, nor bear them meekly. They live in small quarters now and she does her own work. I think there is little affection in their home. We go over to spend the evening soon. Her fashionable friends do not trouble her much, altho she is too proud to speak of it.

October 10th

Just a whole month and not an event noted on these pages. They have certainly not been without the events to note, because a great many things have happened. In the first place, Mr. Gedney is lying quite low with typhoid fever. I have turned nurse with my other duties. The town is full of sickness. I have watched with several sick friends.

By is not well. Mrs. Bond is very much worried as the sickness increases.

Last night we were sitting alone, and she was wishing for her husband, when she said, "O! Mollie, write me some verses to send to Jim, just as if you were in my place, all about how much I love and miss him and about the children."

The following will show how vivid my imagination can be when I try. I am called upon quite often to inscribe some sentiment to somebody, valentines, love letters, and such, and don't know but that I can do better for others than for myself. But after all, my heart is in the verses sent to "Jim."

> Thou art not with me, husband dear,
> To soothe my aching heart,
> I miss thy smile and cheering voice
> That bids dull care depart.
> But memory brings thee back to me,

As in the days of old,
When fondly sitting on thy knee
I heard love's story told,
Or felt thy warm kiss on my cheek
When each felt words too deep to speak.

* * * * *

I would thou wert with us again.
'Twould cheer our lonely hearth,
And gladden us as summer's rain
Makes glad the scorching earth;
O! come to me when balmy sleep
Steals o'er me in a dream of bliss,
When angels their sweet vigils keep,
And press upon my lips a kiss.
I listen for your answer in our home so still,
And hear the gentle echo, "Love, I will."

When I think of the subject of these lines, I cannot help being amused. Mr. Bond is old-fashioned and matter-of-fact, without a shadow of sentiment in his nature, and Mrs. Bond is an easy-going domestic woman, who would as soon think of flying to the moon as writing verses. I wonder what "Jim" will think when these "gushing" lines reach him? I would not be at all surprised to see him arrive by the next boat. For Mrs. Bond said, "I told him *I* wrote them." If there is *any* glory attached to them she is welcome. O! dear, I wish I could write something that would satisfy me, after it is written.

October 30th

Since I last visited you, my little book, I have passed through quite an ordeal. By had not been feeling well for some time, and feared he was threatened with typhoid fever. He came over one evening to see me, and had only been in the house a little while when he was taken violently ill.

There was no one to send for a physician, and knowing his case to be urgent, I went myself, over cross lots and thro alleys, *anyway* to reach Dr. Bradway's office quickly. He had just driven to the door on the return of a trip to the country, so I jumped into the buggy and he drove back in haste, none too soon, for By was almost in convulsions. We worked with him till near morning, before he was relieved, and for days he was considered dangerous. I was his nurse almost constantly, and Dr. Bradway said, "Sanford, if you never loved this girl before, you should love her now, for she has saved your life." One of the girls said, "How *could* you take care of him? *I* couldn't have done it for anything." During By's sickness Mrs. Bond's children were sick. Mr. George was convalescing, so altogether we had a regular hospital. By is only able to be around now. Mrs. Bond has shown herself a kind friend to us both. Last week Dr. Campbell came in to see Mrs. Bond. He was telling of a bad case he had, that of Mrs. Bradford, wife of our representative to Congress.* She has some nervous trouble, and her friends feared she would lose her mind, she was so despondent. She is boarding and [has] no one in particular to be with her. She is not down in bed, but the doctor said she must be gotten out of her state of mind. All at once, he said, "Why, Miss Mollie, you're the very one I want. Put on your things and go with me." At first I said, "No," but she being a sister to Mr. Cole, who had shown me so much kindness during my school term, I thought better of it and went. "All she wants," said Dr., "is someone to 'gab' to her and keep her mind off from herself, and I don't know of anyone that has a better gift of that article than yourself." I stayed

---

* Allen M. Bradford served in three sessions of the Nebraska territorial legislature. While there he engineered the remarkable feat of repealing the criminal code, leaving Nebraska without criminal law until the next session of the legislature. He moved to Colorado in 1860, where in 1862 he became a member of the Territorial Supreme Court and 1865 delegate to Congress from Colorado.

with her five days, and while I perhaps benefited her, I found it quite pleasant for myself and really had a rest. She had lovely rooms, nice books, and was as entertaining to me as I was to her. I rubbed her thoroughly night and morning and that was about all I had to do. She called me her "Magnetic Healer," and I have been thinking which one of my several vocations I would follow, that of *cook, general bottle washer, milk maid, school marm, seamstress, nurse,* or *Poetess!* Mrs. Bradford gave me a $5.00 gold piece, so it seems *Healer Magnetic* is the most remunerative, for that is as much as I earn in two weeks of constant stitching. Beside, I have made a life-long friend and helped Dr. Campbell dispose of a difficult case, for which *he* no doubt received five times as much. I am through at Mrs. Bond's, and as soon as By is able we are going out home. In the meantime have made arrangements to come in two weeks to sew for Mrs. Judge Bailey. I seem to be in demand, and wish I had four hands instead of two.

Hazel Dell
November 5th

By brought me home the first of the week. Will I ever forget those lovely rides over the prairie! We can talk over our plans and have such nice visits. We have never had any particular time set for our marriage, but now if all is well and nothing happens to prevent, we will be married on the 14th of Feb.

Our Uncle Milton and Aunt Eliza are at Grandpa's on a visit. My Uncle is a Methodist minister, and he has had to leave the conference to recuperate his health. They will spend the winter, and will be a great addition to the society. Uncle will preach to the heathen, holding services at Grandpa's house.

We are in receipt of letters from the friends in Indiana. An Uncle and Aunt have met with a double bereavement within the past few months, the loss of two sweet children. They had written a full account of how at the death of the first they felt so rebellious, but more resigned when the last was taken away. This Uncle and Aunt were very dear to me in early life. I wrote them a letter of condolence, and sent some verses I wrote one evening.

Yes! I believe heaven is full of cherubs and cherubims. They only go before to prepare the way.

We are all fast rushing to eternity. We go with the tide, not fully realizing with what velocity we are speeding with [?] many the scenes and strife of this world swallow up all thought of a preparation for the future. Death reminds us of duty. O! that we may think of these things more seriously.

November 20th

We are having quiet times. Aunt Eliza and Cousin Hattie are here a great deal. Hattie is a dainty little thing, about 16, quiet and retiring. The boys are like all others of their kind, full of mischief and fun. Their boys and ours make the welkin ring. Aunt E. thinks this about out of the world. (It is pretty near.) There don't seem to be very much that is *funny* happening, or worth recording.

Perhaps I do not *feel* as funny as I used to, too much *else* to think of, perhaps. Perhaps it is time I was *settling*, anyhow. I don't suppose I will ever be as free from care as I was the first year out here. I must share those of my dear parents. With the hard times and poor crops, and little work and less pay, we cannot be as flourishing as we would wish, but I never say anything to anyone. *I* shall not be the one to grumble or complain. I started out to be a heroine, and must not spoil it all. I must carry out my theories in practice.

Aunt Eliza wonders why *I* don't try to captivate Mr. Tucker, as he is rich. She does not think him as nice-looking as By, but then! he *owns a farm*, and bless my old darling, he don't own much of anything except those lots and—myself. My Aunt likes money, but *she* married for love. I remember or I have heard the folks tell of how my Uncle came to preach in my Grandfather's schoolhouse, a poor circuit preacher without a dollar to his name, and too young to have achieved any fame. Now they are all right, so it is not always just how one starts out in life. A poor beginning makes a good ending, and if we do begin life's voyage poor, we will show what brave hearts can do.

December 1st

I find it very pleasant here at Mrs. Bailey's. The Judge is a jolly man, and his wife gentle and refined. They have three little children. Mr. Bailey is a general merchant. I don't know how he got the name of "Judge," unless because he is fat and jolly. Mr. George Sroat and Mr. Font Pearman are two gentlemen that clerk in the store and board with the family. Sroat is a Kentuckian, tall and angular, while Mr. Pearman must weigh 200. They are both nice, Sroat a bachelor and Pearman a widower and Kentuckian too, so I must look out for that, remembering some of my past experiences. Well, they all know that I am an engaged young lady, and as such I must be very discreet. By is over in Iowa, superintending the making of a canal or ditch. We will not see much of each other for a while, but I hear from him often. Mr. Pearman has a sister living not very far away, Mrs. Decker. I have called upon her several times. Mr. Decker is my class leader, when I go to class, which I confess is not very often, but I am so near the church now I can go more often. I need more grace every day.

December 17th

This is my 21st birthday. I should so have loved to have been at home. I know my Mother's heart is with me today. I was born near *her* 21st birthday. Away back in a little log cabin in an Indiana village on the "Ohio," I first opened my eyes on this world. I have heard my Mother tell of the big, grey, wondering eyes of her baby *Mary*, to *her* the sweetest that ever gazed into a fond Mother's face. O! have I fulfilled the fruition of my parents' hopes? I shall miss their birthday caresses. May Heaven bless and keep the dear parents I love so well.

December 25th

Home for Christmas, to stay 2 weeks. Uncle Milton came in for me. We had a nice ride. He is an entertaining man. We were all together for Christmas dinner. I shall be too busy to write much these days. The weather is fine for this time of year, and I want to enjoy every hour of my time at home, for I leave again soon. All are well and happy, and I wish that I might ever be with them.

January 10th[?], 1860

Back at Mrs. Bailey's. I seem to gravitate between town and country. The road that at one time seemed so long now only appears a pleasant drive. There are several farms opened in the high prairies where people expect to grow timber, so all available land is taken. On New Year's Eve Father came out from town, bringing Mr. George Sroat and his cousin, Mr. Drake, or rather, they brought *him*. He invited them, as he said, "on his own hook." I was glad to see them of *course*, but had expected By, who failed to put in an appearance, which rather dampened my feelings. It was a good opportunity for me to come back, only a little sooner than I had expected. When we got to Bailey's, my first greeting was, "Why! Mollie! you and George married? Who would have believed it?" And sure enough, the report was rife that we were married. George looked all the colors of the rainbow while I bleached several shades, for I thought what if By should hear it! It was known that Father and George went out to our home, that we had a big dinner, and that I came back with him. We had seen Judge Bailey out on the prairie several miles. He had galloped ahead and I suppose for fun (or he said he believed it) had circulated the report. I felt sort of uneasy until I saw By, and he said he felt "streaked" enough. He was too unwell to come out on New Year's. He goes back to Iowa again.

A series of revival meetings are in progress at our church. I shall attend, and by mutual agreement Mr. Sroat or Mr. Pearman go with me, and if By hears any more reports, maybe he will stay at home and go with me himself. It is a source of regret with me that By does not go to church regularly. He is strictly moral, but O! how I wish he were religious. The time is fast approaching when perhaps I can have more influence with him.

On the 20th of this month I go to sew for Mrs. Judge Holly* for three weeks, and then home to be married! ! !

February 1st

I am duly installed at Mrs. Holly's. They have quite a family. It is my very first work for strangers, and I find her rather more exacting than my former patrons, but it won't last long, and I can stand it. Judge Holly is a veritable judge, is a lawyer of some repute, and, while not handsome, is a very affable gentleman. I have heard that his wife is insanely jealous, but I've no time to bother about that. The Grandmother Holly is quite aged, but one of the sweetest old ladies I've ever met. One is made to feel their subordinate position more in a family like this. I spend my Sundays again with Mrs. Preston. I went to see Mrs. Burnham the

---

*Charles F. Holly was an attorney for Russell, Majors, and Waddell. In 1860 he went to Colorado and operated a stamp mill (see p 132). He served in the Colorado legislature in 1861, and in 1865 became Chief Justice of the Colorado Supreme Court.

other day. She gave me some beautiful embroidered under-sleeves and handkerchiefs for wedding presents. She told me so much of her affairs. While I feel so sorry for her, I fear she has brought some of her troubles upon herself by not being more domestic, and perhaps a little vain. They are quite reduced in circumstances.

But two or three of my friends know that I am to be married this month. There has been so many comments on the affair, as there always are about long engagements. Ours will be a very quiet wedding. The distance, and time of year, makes it impossible for many of my town friends to come. I have been up to ask Cousin Anna. The stepmother is still there. I have no use for her. At one time she tried to make trouble between By and I. There were two or three letters exchanged that had better not have been written, some few weeks of misunderstanding that I never even chronicled here. I would not mar these pages with an account of it, but soon all was made right, and with that *one* exception our courtship has run smoothly, notwithstanding the adage that the "course of *true* love never runs smoothly."

I have no doubts or misgivings in regard to him. I trust him fully and truly. I trust we may enter this new life in the right spirit. Just as thou art, my darling, I take thee. Just as I am thou takest me. We promise to love in prosperity or adversity.

Saturday, February 11th

Uncle Milton came in to "town" and brought By and I out home. We were at Mrs. Preston's, who did so many little things for me. I am glad the weather is so nice, and hope the skies will be clear until after next Tuesday. I want everything to be propitious for the event that takes place on that day.

Monday night, February 13th

This is the last time I shall write in this journal as Mollie Dorsey, and there are a few thoughts I must inscribe. My heart is full, so full, that I scarce know how to express them. It is no little thing to leave the home that has been so dear to me, and I can realize it is something of a trial for my parents. I can catch a look occasionally, not reproachful, but earnest and endearing. I know were it in their power they would shield me from all of care and trials there is in the future. I know this is a solemn step, one that involves a lifetime of happiness or misery, but I am only carrying out the divine law, to leave father and mother and cleave unto my husband, and I go into this with implicit faith in my chosen one. I have been looking over the past, and can say that no ghost of a lover rises up to reproach me with infidelity. The house is still. All are asleep long ago, but my thoughts are too busy to sleep tonight.

> Alone, within my room by this old window seat
> Where falls the pale moon's softening ray,
> I sit and count the hours with heart beats quick
> That ushers in my wedding day.
>
> I break all slighter bonds that once I may have made,
> I feel no shadowy doubts or fears,
> I *know* all earlier passions pale and fade
> Before *this* love of my maturer years.
>
> I do not doubt thee, darling—for I know thy love
> As pure and true, as that I give to thee.
> But fervently as prayers I send above,
> I ask thee, search thy heart tonight for me.
>
> And canst thou now as pure a record show?
> O! do not hide from me a part.

My heart would break! 'twould be a cruel blow
To know that I was second in thy heart.

I do not ask again. I do not seek to hear
What thou hast been within the past.
I risk it all, my heart shall know no fear,
I know that thou art mine as long as life shall last.

By is away tonight. He and brother Sam took Grandpa's
horses and went to Tecumseh, the county seat, to procure
the license, since that legal document is necessary in this
Territory to fasten the nuptial knot. We were a little surprised to see Sam return about 4 o'clock alone. It seems the
County Clerk, whose business is to issue the aforesaid, was
absent. In fact, his trip was to get blanks for this very thing,
as he had been newly elected to office. It was uncertain
when he would return, but was expected every hour. So
to keep us from being uneasy at any delay, Sam came home.
I had hoped By would be here yet tonight, but it is too late
now, and he will no doubt be here bright and early in the
morning. Two carriage loads came this afternoon. Mr. Sam
Harris from Neb. City brought cousin Anna. Mr. George
Gedney came with a friend.

But I must to rest, if I wish to get any beauty sleep tonight. I baked my own wedding cake and everything is prepared for the wedding at 2 o'clock P.M. tomorrow. Other
friends around are coming, and to give *them* a chance to
get home the same day we have made this arrangement to
be married early in the day.

Sabbath P.M., *February 19th, 1860*

Finds me a happy bride. Our wedding did not pass
as quietly as I anticipated. Tuesday morning we were busy
with preparations for dinner, receiving and entertaining our
guests, and it is something to do that in as small quarters as
we occupy. We were looking for By every moment, but

after 10 o'clock I began to feel nervous, for he had had plenty of time to come, it seemed. I dreaded to have the appointed hour pass without the ceremony. Twelve! One! Two! Three! o'clock came, and no bridegroom. Many jokes were indulged in at my expense. I was fluctuating between hope and fear, but never doubting but that he was unavoidably delayed. Gedney came to me and said, "Some of these chaps are slippery" (he never did like By) "and I tell *you* I'd have got here if I *died* trying to" (the last with a tragic emphasis). At three o'clock the folks were about starved. The dinner was overdone, and it was decided we "eat, drink, and be merry." Mr. Harris proposed being groom by proxy. We all *tried* to be gay. Father and Mother looked grave and anxious. After the dinner was ended and evening approached, I could hardly stand the suspense. I would steal off and weep and pray, and come to the house and smile and be gay. The young folks played games in the sitting room, while the older ones sat around the kitchen fire, regaling each other, for my especial benefit, with harrowing incidents where the bridegrooms *never* came, and the brides ended their days in insane asylums.

The dear old Grandpa meekly suggested that "Fox" was a fine animal, that *Byron* was an honest young man (or we had thought he was) and that stranger things had happened than—that—but he did not finish his remarks, for I retorted with spirit that By was no horse thief, or, if he was, that he as would soon run off with a calf, as poky old Fox. After this the poor old gentleman sighed and groaned the hours away until 8 o'clock, when he thought he had better go home and to bed. So to make peace witn him, and to take another season of weeping and praying, I took him up to the house, and helped him to bed. Then went out once more to listen. I heard the sounds of horse's hoofs, and rushing to the roadside, I saw in the bright starlight my truant lover. His first exclamation was: "My gracious, Mollie, what do they think?" I said, "What do you suppose *I* think, Lord Byron?" He was nearly frozen, so we hurried into the house, while Bro. Sam, who too was on the lookout, cared for old "Fox," and the dear Grandpa's fears were at rest. I made some tea and, while he was thawing out, he told of his meanderings, and we made a little plan to have some sport out of what had so far been a prosy affair. Our wedding garments were down at the house, By's in his valise hanging behind the door, and mine in a small trunk also in the room where the young folks were. We would have to get them out without exciting suspicion, get them up to the other house, dress, and suddenly appear before them and have the ceremony over before they could recover from their surprise, for everyone had given him up for the night. Father, Mother, Uncle, Aunt, Grandma, and Bro. Sam were all that were in the secret. I came in and said I would join in a game, and look no more for my faithless lover, at which I had an approving glance from Mr. Gedney. In flying around I accidentally knocked the valise down. Bro. Sam was on hand to take it away. After a little I stumbled over the trunk and someone said that's a nuisance, so it was shoved into the other room. As soon as I could I got out of the play and went up to the house, where we dressed quickly as possible, helping each other with the finishing touches of our toilets. In the meanwhile Mother and Aunt had arranged the room. We came and stood outside the door, ready for the signal from Uncle Milton. Aunt stepped into where the company were, and said, "We will not wait for Mr. Sanford any longer. Come out to prayers." All marched solemnly into the kitchen. At a signal, the door opened, and stepping in, the ceremony was immediately begun, and Byron N. Sanford and Mary E. Dorsey were made man and wife together. Such a storm as followed, kisses and exclamations of surprise. Some of the best of the dinner had been preserved, and willing hands soon had a wedding supper, with a genuine Bride and Groom at their posts of honor.

And we were married in the kitchen! Start not! ye fairy brides. Beneath your veils and orange blossoms, in some home where wealth and fashion congregate, *your* vows are no truer, your heart no happier, than was this maiden's, in the kitchen of a log cabin, in the wilderness of Nebraska. Time may change, and I may have more attractive surroundings, and I may smile at this primitive wedding. I only trust my heart may ever be as brave and true as then and as happy as now. We are having a quiet honeymoon. By is not very well and will remain a while. Our plans are not definite. Father would like us to settle on a farm, but perhaps By may go to some other place where there is a better prospect for beginners.

Dora went home with Coz Anna and Mr. Harris to visit Mrs. Tucker where Father is boarding in town. Mr. Harris is a co-worker with Father in the shop, and a gentleman he likes very much.

Little Book, I wonder if I will journalize as much now! They say the romance fades from one's life after marriage. To be sure there hasn't been much in my girlhood, but then, I can make it full of good deeds, my *home* a haven of rest and peace. *The Lord help and bless me.* By and I took a long walk over the prairies this afternoon, just to be to ourselves. The day has been lovely for the time of year. Arm in arm we trod the russet grass, the soft grey light above, and away off to the west the sky was banked with golden clouds in the coming sunset. Was it typical? Starting as we are with not the brightest surroundings, will they still lead on to brightness and glory? And will the end of our pilgrimage be the brightest?

March 1st

Weather very disagreeable, "Coming in like a lion."

Shrill winds blow the falling snow. We all have colds. I have neuralgia. Fortunate for me this swollen *jaw* did not decorate my visage on my wedding day. By has has several carbuncles on his back, so if these afflictions combined are not enough to dissipate the romance, I'm mistaken. We have a letter from Father. He tells us that Mr. Harris seems quite taken with Dora, seriously, *he* thinks. I am glad the dear girl is having some pleasure. Uncle Milton's have worried so much about Grandpa's living out here in their old age, and have persuaded them to move into Neb. City. Uncle Chas. has been out to visit us all. Uncle George is off out west *somewhere*, so plenty of changes will soon take place. Nan declares she will leave or do something desperate. She has to work harder than ever before, and don't enjoy it very much.

Friday, March 9th

"Wonders never cease," and little Journal, I've some startling news to record today. Nothing worse tho than the marriage of Sister Dora to Mr. Sam Harris. Father came out home on Friday to tell the news and prepare us for the event. On Saturday Mr. Harris came with Dora. Father had supplied her with the necessary articles for her trousseau, limited enough, poor young one. We visited Sunday, and became more acquainted, and all like Mr. Harris, altho dear Mother could hardly feel reconciled to the suddenness of the affair. On Monday all hands turned in, Aunt Eliza and Cousin Hattie assisting, to prepare "Eudora" for the nuptials. The wedding gown was to be made, besides other articles. Her dress was a pretty shade of blue merino, and made by myself, and "if *I do* say it as shouldn't," it is a marvel of beauty and fit, altho I was suffering with my poor face all the time. On Tuesday Mr. Harris and "Bro. Sam" went for the license, and returned the same day. By Thursday morning the sewing was all done. Then the wedding cake was baked and preparations made for the supper. There were no guests, as we had no time, nor did they desire any extra work. At 8 o'clock they were quietly married by Uncle Milton. Not a shadow of romance about the whole affair, unless the "love at first sight" might be called such, for their first acquaintance was at my wedding three weeks ago. There wasn't even a "hitch or a jar" in the proceedings, everything passing off as "serene as a summer's morning." Mr. Harris does not believe in long engagements, and beside, they wished Uncle Milton to "tie the knot." The family leave in a few days for Indiana, all very much improved in health, and since he has disposed of two of the brood, my dear Aunt E. will have less to worry about, for she is one of those that believes in early marriages and is called something of a matchmaker. She certainly made a good one for herself, for my Uncle is splendid in every way.

Monday, March 12th

Tonight the house seems deserted. Sam and Dora, with Father, left on Saturday, and today By went with Uncle Milton's folks as far as Neb. City. All we have to do is to gather up the tangled threads, adjust domestic matters, and talk over the past two weeks' events. My marriage was a theme of comment for so long, *two whole years almost*, and came off as a matter of course, but Dora's we can hardly realize to have been at all. Mother will feel *my* loss more keenly on account of her going. Dora is a great comfort to Mother. She has been a dutiful and good child. My Father calls her "Fidelity."

March 20th

I have letters from my darling. He is hurrying to finish the contract on the ditch and will come back to me. Last night we had two strangers, gentlemen from "Pikes

Peak" or Denver, stop for the night. Mr. George West,* editor of [a] paper in [the] small town of Golden near Denver, was one of them, or *the* one, rather, that has given me the Pikes Peak fever. He says, "Don't think of going anywhere else but to Denver. There are openings there for young beginners. There are thousands now crossing the plains. There are good gold diggings out there." I have written a letter to By to come home and make arrangements to go, and I will stay here until he can send for me, for I suppose we could hardly both go. Mr. West says he can make $8 or $10 per day at his trade.

April 1st

I came in town when Grandpa's moved their goods, and have helped them get settled in their new home. I called today on Mrs. Clark, an acquaintance, who is preparing to go to Denver with her husband, who is freighting across the plains. She has made me more anxious than ever, and Mr. Clark wants to make arrangements for us both to go with them. A great many Neb. City people are already there and others going. Sam Harris will go, and not without Dora, so that makes me more anxious than ever to go. They are boarding at Mrs. Tucker's.

April 5th

By has returned, and we are boarding at Mrs. Clark's. Have about decided to go to Denver. By has rented a shop to do repairing. Business is good just now, as so many are getting up their outfits to cross the plains, and passing thro

* George West, a Boston newspaper man, came to Colorado in 1859 and was one of the founders of the town of Golden, where he published the *Western Mountaineer*. He was on his way back to Boston for more printing equipment when he stopped at the Dorsey farm and persuaded Mollie that Colorado held the future of By and herself. After Civil War Service, West established the *Colorado Transcript* at Golden and was its long-time editor and publisher.

here on their way from other points. If we can possibly make arrangements we will go. Our folks are quite willing for me to go. My health has not been good since I taught school, and they think the trip will do much for me.

April 8th

The "die is cast," and we go to Denver in company with the Clarks, whether it be for weal or woe, we do not know. The distance from the Missouri River is about 700 miles over the great American desert. The trip probably will take as many weeks, as we are to travel with oxen. Mrs. Clark has a span of ponies and light wagon. The freight goes in a large wagon, and she and I are to drive the ponies. By has laid in 6 months' supplies, bought a small cook stove, a few housekeeping articles, and some clothing. Mr. Clark carries our freight for the assistance By gives him in driving the cattle. Two yoke of cows and one yoke of cattle or oxen. Dora and Sam have started ahead, but we will probably overtake them, but Mr. Harris, with his usual rush, cannot wait. By some means, and I hardly know how, Mr. Daily is to go as guide, a part of the way. Mrs. Burnham's brother Ned, a boy of 18, is also going along. Nan has been in town for a few days visiting a friend. She has made the acquaintance of Mr. Henry Harvey, and they will go with us as far as Father's, where we will stop a few days to rest up and get started right. I have no time for writing.

CHAPTER SIX

Across the Plains

April 12, 1860—June 24, 1860

Hazel Dell, April 12th

We left Neb. City late Monday afternoon, started out all right, with good-bys and good wishes from a host of friends. We came three miles and camped and had a little introduction to camp life. The men are green hands at driving cattle, and such a time as they had, whoaing and hawing themselves hoarse, and almost upsetting the wagon. The load was too heavy, and the cattle almost refused to go. We were a tired, discouraged set. Mr. Harvey has been with surveying parties and knows all about camping. Mrs. Clark, who all along has been almost angelic, took a "tantrum" (her husband calls it). If this is a sample, I fear a repetition of it. Then when we came home we invited her to stop at the house, but she preferred to stay in her tent, and said so many unkind things and made me feel so dependent, that we held a "council of war" and almost gave up going at all. Our traps were perhaps just that much too much for the load. Only for Mr. Clark we would not go.

But By found a man that would trade a span of mares for his town lot. The whole load was unpacked and our things put to themselves, which should have been done at first. Mrs. Clark does not like me to stay at the house at all. I feel very sad to leave the dear ones. Years may elapse before we meet again, and some of us perhaps never! "It may be for years, it may be forever." I fear we will not overtake Sam and Dora. Dear Ad cries constantly. Father and Mother give all they can toward fitting us for the journey.

Wednesday, 16th

We are well on our way. We started Wednesday at 2 P.M. The good-bys were sad, and yet they tried to send me off in good spirits. After going a few hundred yards on the road I looked back and saw my little brother Charlie running after the teams, screaming "Sister! Sister!" I got out of the wagon and went back and kissed him again and again! and then watched him trudging back to the house. We had not been an hour on our road, when one of those pitiless storms came, with wind and hail. It was all the men could do to manage the cattle. The oxen are all right, but the cows no doubt felt it an indignity to be yoked up to work, to be expected to do double duty. Mrs. Clark apologized before we started and promised to be more agreeable, but O! dear, it was enough to make us all cross. We had prepared our supplies before starting. "Ned" drives our wagon. We did not have time or opportunity to get a cover, making the trade we did, so the stoves and loose things are hauled in that, and our boiler of victuals were on that wagon and far in the rear. We had to camp on wet ground, wet wood, and not much supper, and beside I was sick, but finally we went to sleep and awoke in the morning to find it clear and warm, and started out again. We are camped at Beatrice tonight on the "Big Blue," a lovely spot. Mother gave me a half-dozen fine hens and a rooster. We had them in a coop behind the big wagon. In crossing the river this evening, the water came into it, and the poor rooster will not herald the coming dawn for us again, as he was drowned. We thought all had met the same fate. This is our first disaster, and as I hear hens are worth five dollars in Denver and roosters double that, I naturally feel sorry. "Count not your chickens!"

Friday, 17th

We came 10 miles today. Are camped on Cub Creek. Road has been hilly. We see a few cultivated farms. All feel better, but a little nervous as we hear there are robbers abroad. The men have fixed their ammunition handy, but if we all get to sleep I guess they will not use it, but the cattle are to be kept close in to camp. Minnie, Mrs. C., is improving. She has asked me to call her Minnie henceforth.

Saturday, 18th

Travelled 22 miles today, and all are tired. Were out of sight of timber all day. We see immense trains off on the St. Joe road. Are camped on "Little Sandy," a small stream with high grassy banks and running thro a bed of white sand. Felt like taking off my shoes and stockings and wading through it.

Sunday, 19th

The first on the plains. It is decided we "lay by" of Sundays, but after all we don't rest much, for we have to roast and bake, and clean up generally, as the men will not stop of week days. I find camping not adapted to journalizing, but I will try to write a little almost every day. There are 6 of us to cook for. Mr. Daily generally goes ahead and selects our camping ground. He was out here last year and knows the country. He never mentions Dora. By and

I took a little ramble this evening. We seldom get a word alone. There is but the one tent and all sleep in that, or we four, Clark and "Minnie," By and I.

Monday, 20th

It is really surprising how time flies. Our pace seems slow enough. Minnie and I travel in the rear, and far enough to keep out of the dust. The men are getting more accustomed to driving, altho the "cows" get obstreperous. I heard By swear at them today, the first time I ever heard a profane word from him. "Minnie" called me a fool for crying. The road is full of teams. Tonight the camps are thick around us. The dust is dreadful! We begin to see where the *"novelty"* comes in. This camp is on the "Little Blue." We found a spring of ice cold water. We almost suffer during the day for good water to drink.

Tuesday, 21st

Up this morning before the dawn. We will pass mail stations or ranches now every 10 or 15 miles. The stage coach runs from St. Joe to Denver, carrying passengers and mail. When the coaches pass us on the road, I imagine the passengers look with eyes of pity on us poor plodding pilgrims. I sent a letter home today.

Sunday, 26th

Are near to Fort Kearney, a military post. See lots of soldiers. The land here is not cultivated. Stock graze on the seemingly bare prairies. Emigration is immense. We hear that 70,000 persons have already passed over this route going west. Have reached the Platte River, a low sluggish stream with low bare banks and full of sandy islands. The men went hunting today. The ducks they brought in proved to be only mud hens. "Minnie" has not spoken to me today. We were alone in the tent all the afternoon, so I have had plenty of time for meditation.

April 28th

We had a terrific wind storm last night, and all day we had to lay by. This makes the men uneasy and Minnie cross. I laid on the floor of the tent and rested all I could. Tonight my candle flares so I cannot write.

April 29th

Started at daybreak this morning to make up for lost time. We average 20 miles a day, but travel late and early. The scenery is monotonous. Some cottonwood and willow timber on the river. High bluffs rise on either side that look majestic in the distance but grow meagre as we approach them.

Thursday, 31st *

We have come along at a good pace today. Were overtaken by Mr. Henry Brown of Neb. City today. He said he would "give all the gold in Pikes Peak to see his wife and boy." We hear conflicting reports about the mountains. Some are returning for their families, while others are shaking the dust of Denver from their feet, and cursing the place and the people. This eve a poor fellow asked to be kept over night. He had got lost from his train by starting out to hunt for buffalo. Suffice to say he found no buffalo, but spent several hours picking the prickly pears from his swollen feet, and wishing himself back in New York. The river here is clear of islands, and looks like a broad silver lake in the moonlight.

* The entry dates at this point are incorrect, possibly due to an error in copying when Mollie transcribed the journal. The month of May is omitted.

Friday, June 1st

Seventy-five miles from Ft. Kearney. I walked 3 miles today and helped By drive the cattle, as "Minnie" wanted Mr. Clark to ride with her. I wish I could walk *all* the way. Tonight we find no wood. Have to burn willow switches. Traveled 18 miles thro alkali dust and prickly pears.

Saturday, 2nd

Passed an Indian village this afternoon. The creatures looked too filthy to live. They are dreadful beggars, and if they cannot get what they ask for, will steal. Stopped a while at Gilman's ranch, a Neb. City man.* They live in an adobe house, but have a splendid well of water, and I think more of that than I would of seeing a mansion. We find good water at all of the ranches.

Sunday, 3rd

"Cottonwood Springs." ** Laid by to rest. I would give a great deal if there was more congeniality between Mrs. Clark and I. "Minnie" was too sick this morning to ride in "our" little wagon. She preferred to lie on the mattress in the larger one, as the slow, steady pace of the oxen was more conducive to comfort and rest. So for *once* I was mistress of the ponies.

They are so full of life early in the mornings that we generally drive ahead a mile or so to cool them down,

---

* John K. Gilman and his brother Jeremiah operated a ranche on the Oregon Trail about fifteen miles east of Cottonwood Springs. They sold supplies to travelers, freighted, and carried on a fur trade with the Sioux and Cheyenne.

** Cottonwood Springs, located a short distance from the forks of the Platte, was a well-known point on the trail. A military post, Camp McKean, later called Fort McPherson, was established at the site in 1863.

then drive back and take our line of march in the rear of the "caravan." This morning they were unusually "frisky." I gave them the reins, and we cantered ahead at a lively rate. The air was bracing, the roads smooth and hard, and I was enjoying it hugely. Coming down into a ravine where the road curved, what was my horror to come upon a squad of Indian warriors! They immediately surrounded me, and began their gibberish of "Wano Squaw," "Wano White Squaw" (good Squaw), evidently amused at my consternation. For a wonder the ponies were quiet, perhaps as paralyzed as myself. I wear my hair in two long braids for comfort and convenience. An Indian seized hold of each one, took their hunting knives and made every demonstration of cutting them off, *or* scalping, I did not know which. But after almost scaring me to death, they released their hold, and began peeking and poking around in the wagon.

I knew they were fond of sugar. Our box had been filled before starting, so I opened it, gasping, "Help yourselves, gentlemen"—which they did—entirely emptying it, eating all they could and tying the remainder in the corners of their dirty blankets. Appreciating my generosity, they began then a howl for "Becskit, Becskit." Immediately the bread box was thrown open, and the noon-day lunch that we always carry in our wagon went the way of the sugar. What might have happened next, no one knows, but the distant echo of the welcome "Whoa. Haw. Gee" came over the hill, and brandishing their whips and knives, the pesky redskins gave war whoop, and galloped away. I turned my ponies, now thoroughly frightened, and sped back to the wagons, almost frantic with excitement. Ned was for following them. As he cannot shoot an antelope, he would be satisfied with an Indian.

Hereafter I shall meekly follow in the rear. No more

thrilling encounters for me on this trip. The Indians are peaceable, I suppose, but are too treacherous to trust out alone!

It rained hard all the afternoon, making traveling very laborious. Tonight everything is wet, and everyone cross and used up. It is almost beyond human endurance at such times as these to keep amiable, but I do try very hard, as Minnie says, "Try to be a saint," but fail. O! dear! O! dear! I'll be one when I get to heaven.

This is Sunday again. We are taking a much-needed rest, and drying out our damp clothes after the storm. A funny incident or accident happened last night, not so "funny" either to By and Clark. Sometime in the night, By got up to get a drink of water. I heard him "spluttering" and "muttering," saying, "That tastes queer." Clark called out "I thought so too." Lighting a candle, he found he had drank of the water I had rinsed his muddy socks in, instead of the water pail.

The boys acknowledged that "dirt was healthy," but they preferred dealing out their own doses. They will not prowl around the tent in the dark again, nor will I, poor culprit, leave dirty water to entrap them. If we get through this trip without being "scalped" or "pizened," I'll be glad. This is a fair example of the "novelty" and "romance" of a trip across the plains that one reads about. Let all try it who are thirsting for the romantic. I just expect to find my head almost white before we get to Denver. But there's no turning back now. Minnie is better today, and more amiable than for some time. The men went off hunting antelope. The evening is so lovely, and I would enjoy talking, but she has the "pouts," so I have come to my journal from whence comes no rebuff. She said today, "O! you're trying to be literary but you can't," and surely the record of the past few weeks don't show me to have made a success. Too bad we cannot have harmony. In the evening's quiet hour we review the past day's events and see where we have made mistakes, and we resolve to profit by them, but perhaps the next day we repeat the same. I am glad I did not quarrel with Minnie today as she seemed determined I should. I feel subdued, and calm, and as the dreamy south wind fans my brow, my heart goes back to the old home I love so well. *Sweet "Hazel Dell."*

Monday, 4th

We are still in camp. The "boys" came in late last night with two young antelope. They have been cutting it up and salting it *down*. Minnie became so interested she forgot to be cross. We did up a big baking and are ready to move on tomorrow.

Tuesday, 5th

We had a terrible storm of rain and wind today, with the worst thunder and lightning I ever saw. One is perfectly unprotected on these plains. After it was over and we had come a little way, we passed a fresh grave. A poor fellow was killed by lightning, wagon and contents burnt. Someone had hurriedly scooped a hole and put him in. By the grave his charred hat, and the body of his dog lay. It made me feel so badly. Minnie is sick tonight. I had all the cooking to do, and have bathed her head until she sleeps. I suppose she is not well, and I must have all the charity I can. I don't feel very well myself, but she thinks I am babyish. O! dear! Met Tom Chivington* on his way back. He gives us encouraging accounts. We have only made 10 miles today, but it is that much nearer.

Wednesday

Got along nicely today. Met another Neb. City

* Tom Chivington, the son of John M. Chivington, was a freighter operating between Nebraska City and Denver.

friend, Mr. Mason, on his way back for a load of flour. He had sold a load in Denver for 15 dollars per hundred. He tells us Harris is 75 miles ahead. When Mr. Daily heard that, he took the back track. Now I think he hoped to see her sometime. Passed O'Fallans Bluffs today. The road runs for miles through high bluffs. The feed is scarce. We missed our guide tonight, and have the worst camp on the trip. It rains as I write. By says, "Do come to bed." Minnie is better. We passed more Indians today. It would puzzle our friends to distinguish us from these squaws, if we were dressed as they are, for I believe we are as black.

Sunday again

I am sick myself tonight. Such terrible storms as we have. They come mostly in the night. We are yet 200 miles from Denver, and have the worst part of the road to travel yet. With this comforting (?) thought I'll hie me to slumber.

Monday

I find it is almost impossible to write. I only do it to keep dates and incidents, and don't even do that. Everything went wrong today. The cattle cut up all sorts of capers. The men raved, and Mr. Clark swore a torrent of oaths. My tears had the effect of keeping By from it, as I've heard no more swearing from him since that day, but really it is aggravating how those "critters" do act. Mr. Clark and Minnie had a quarrel. She threw herself into my arms and had hysterics. She had been scolding "Ned," and he had threatened to leave. I kept amiable, and succeeded in restoring peace, and tonight Clark is holding Minnie in his arms. Ned and I cooked the supper. He *hates* the "Madame" in general.

12th

Our road today was through sand, almost to the wagon hubs. I walked almost all day. The cattle walked quietly, and Mr. Clark drove for Minnie. The land to which we are travelling should surely be one of "milk and honey" to repay us poor pilgrims for these long dreary marches. An old fellow came into camp this eve. He said, "My dear wimmen, you'll rue to your dyin' day ever havin' sot your feet on that thar miserable Pikes Peak." The "Peak" I believe is a high mountain one hundred miles from Denver, so I guess we won't "sot" our feet there very soon. Half the people we see are heading for Pikes Peak. On one covered wagon I see lettered, "Pikes Peak or bust," and on one returning, "Pikes Peak and busted."

We saw large herds of antelope today and some buffalo across the river.

Thursday, 14th

I have been a bride four months tonight, but I'm too tired to expatiate much about it. The weather is so hot and we are so dusty and dirty. In fact we are about sick, all of us. Even the cattle and ponies seem drowsy. We have decided to rest for one day. Rest? Where *is* rest for us!

Friday, 15th

The way our men folks have rested was to hunt antelope. Mr. Clark is like a schoolboy. If there is one in sight Ned uses his revolver, uses up his ammunition but has his first game to bring down, but By and Clark came in with two, so we are provided with fresh meat. We fed a poor forlorn pilgrim today. He got away with three quarts of milk. Our cows furnish us with plenty of that article. Ned would like to live on this very spot forever, where he could have antelope every day. He would get clear of his ammunition sure.

June 16th

We have seen large bands of Indians today. One old "Buck" tried to "swap" some ponies to By for his white squaw, but By said the poor fellow had never done him any harm. The "joke" was all well enough but perfectly lost upon the Indian. The stern realities are rather taking the jokes out of him, and the poetry out of me. If we only had more pleasant companions. Mr. Clark would be nice, but his wife worries him to death. We have met at least a hundred teams today on the homeward track, mostly Missourians. They denounce the country as a "fraud" because they could not pick up gold on the streets. The gold excitement is what takes thousands there. But *we* are not expecting much!

June 19th

One of the hottest days I ever felt, but the road has been like a pavement, hard and smooth. We are camping on Bear Creek, a small creek coming from the prairie and emptying into the Platte. The road is high up from the river and not much grass. Plenty of prickly pears and cactus.

Wednesday, 20th

This evening we came down on a broad plaza or flat, where the grass is fresh and green. The sight was grand after so much dreary road. Hundreds of camps are around us. The cattle browsing on the fresh, tender grass seem to enjoy it as much as we. Here we met some more Neb. friends.

Thursday noon, "Fremonts Orchard"

Here am I beneath the shade of a towering cottonwood tree. The most of the trees here are small and look like apple trees, why, I suppose, General Fremont named it "orchard." I have been feasting my eyes upon this enchant-ing scene. Steep high bluffs surround this little spot. The grass is soft beneath my feet. Before me glides the sparkling river, studded with its group of pretty islands, and far away to the west I see the blue ridge of the mountains, a view of the "promised land." Their silver-capped peaks rise above like clouds of glory, and from this time on we will not be out of sight of the mountain range landscape.

But a call from the men say, "Up and off again," for we have the worst hill of sand to go through that we have had on the road. Farewell to rhapsodizing, and up to our plod-ding pilgrimage again. We are now nearing Denver, about 75 miles away. We hear that Sam and Dora are living in their tent and awaiting our arrival in Denver. Too bad that we could not have gone together. This is my first experi-ence at not getting along with anyone, but I have heard that a trip like this would try one's friendship. Of course Mrs. Clark was only an acquaintance. I have always prided my-self that I could adapt myself to *anyone*, but I have made a miscrable failure. So many of the Nebraska people we have met have said, "*I* could have told you all about her disagreeableness," but I know she is not well. She makes me feel our dependence. After this I shall ride on our own wagon, out in the broiling sun, and By will drive, and Ned can help Mr. C.

A band of Indians rushed into camp today and stam-peded our cattle. They were either drunk or bent on mis-chief. The men will keep watch tonight.

June 24th

Sunday, but so anxious are we to get through, that we will travel on. We passed the ruins of some old forts or trading posts. The adobe walls have crumbled into Mother Earth. We passed through a camp or Indian village of 200 wigwams. Mercy! I almost fear we will be taken, scalps and all, yet before we get through. I write no more until we are safely housed or tented somewhere. Tomorrow our long march will be ended. I am thankful we are alive. I ought to think more of this than other affairs.

CHAPTER SEVEN

Denver and Gold Hill

June 26, 1860—September 25, 1860

Tuesday, June 26th, 1860

The Promised Land is gained and we are in Denver tonight. We entered the city of the plains at 10 o'clock A.M. We soon found Dora. They are camping on the banks of Cherry Creek, a dry, sandy channel. There are no houses to be had, and hundreds of families are living in wagons, tents, and shelters made of carpets and bedding. I like the looks of the place. Everybody seems glad to welcome the coming pilgrims, as we are called, anybody from "back in the States." It is estimated there are five thousand people in and around Denver. It seems so near the mountains that I thought I could easily walk over there, but Dora says they are 12 miles away. The atmosphere is so dry and clear it brings distant objects nearer.

We will all camp together until we can look around. Dora had lettuce, radishes, and young onions for dinner, a treat to us. I paid 25 cents for a quart of milk. Minnie and I parted friendly, at least. She admitted that she had been ugly, but said she couldn't help it. They sell their load and return in a few days to Nebraska for another. There is more money made freighting than in any other way. Sam has employment at carpentering. By sees no chance to get work at his trade, as the place is overrun, a blacksmith shop on every corner. We have interviewed our mutual pocketbook and found less than five dollars left. But we are supplied with several months' provisions of staple articles. The luxuries we will dispense with. Everything is high here. We see a great many old friends—Judge Bennet * and family live by Dora. They are Neb. people.

July 4th

There has been quite a celebration today by the Masonic and other Orders, and the Sabbath school children. It did me good to see the little ones. The music was fine. The bands play here all the time. The gambling houses employ them. It must be a corrupt place. Fast men and women nearly equal the good.

Sam traded his team for some lots, and he and By are building a board shanty. We are to move as soon as it is finished. It rains every afternoon, a blessing, for it is hot and dusty during the day. The nights are deliciously cool, and one's sleep is refreshing.

Judge Holly from Neb. City called upon us today. He is one of a company bringing a stamp mill to go to the mines in the mountains. He seems interested in our welfare, and will use his efforts to help By into something. Altho the prospect is not flattering, we do not feel discouraged. There seems to be an invigorating and exhilarating effect in the atmosphere here. Then there is so much life and

* Hiram P. Bennet had been one of the founders of Nebraska City and a member of the territorial legislature. He went to Colorado in 1859 and settled in Denver. He served as a delegate to Congress from Colorado 1861-1865 and as postmaster of Denver from 1864 to 1874.

excitement, and I like it and feel hopeful that we will be all right.

July 5th

A letter from home, the dear, dear home, and all are well. A letter comes through in 6 days by express. We pay 25 cents for one, and the same to send one back, so we won't write every day. Well, who should appear upon the scene today but George Gedney. He drove through, and hoped to have overtaken us on the road. Dr. Rankin, another home friend, called and took me a lovely ride, almost to the foot of the mountains.

Sabbath, 9th

We moved into our "mansion" yesterday, for such it seems after living on the ground so long. The room is only 10 by 20, boarded up and down, and not plastered, but we are happy. Now if By has to leave to hunt employment, I can be with my sweet sister. We *need* each other, too.

Monday, 10th

Judge Holly brought a man, a mining man, who has engaged By to go to the mountains if *I* will take some of his men to board. So something *has* "turned up" through the friendly interest of Mr. Holly. Mr. McKnight's mill is near his, at Gold Hill mining district. By is to go down the river to some point to meet a train of wagons of machinery, to intercept them rather, and have them take a shorter cut to the mountains than coming through Denver. He will be gone 4 or 5 days, as he has to walk 25 or 30 miles. I felt as if he were going to be gone a month, such a baby am I, but the country is full of cutthroats and robbers, ready to waylay the unprotected.

Thursday, 12th

I have had a grand time tramping around the country

[133]

today. We went up Cherry Creek four miles and gathered wild currants and gooseberries. We saw men prospecting in the sands of Cherry Creek for gold. It is found in the Platte too, very fine, but in too small quantities to pay well. We hear of discoveries in the mountains. There is water in Cherry Creek after heavy rains on the Divide. That is south of Denver, a high ridge that separates the Platte and Arkansas rivers. Now it is perfectly dry, but by digging down two feet there is found pure cold water. I wonder where my darling is tonight? There is a terrible thunderstorm raging. Heaven protect him is my prayer. I can but feel lonely.

Saturday, 14th

Well, how things do turn out. Yesterday Sam came in and announced that they were going to Central City, a mining town, to stay several months. In a few hours they had packed up and left. He had a chance for a good position at $5.00 per day and could not let it pass. That left me monarch of the premises. When By comes, we are to rent or sell for him. A young lady living across the way will be with me of nights. I have nice neighbors. Dora had a good cry to think she had to leave me, but dear heart, our paths may henceforth be divided. While it is sad to contemplate, it is all we can expect. But our hearts will be true always.

Wednesday, 18th

And By has been gone a week. I am nearly frantic, not knowing what has become of him. I went out today to hunt up some sewing. I must be occupied. A lady nearby is going back to the States and will give me all I can do if I take house hold goods in exchange. I have no money. I almost feel like a lone widow—God knows! *I may* be one now! Some terrible thing may have happened. I heard today of a man down 20 miles that was found dead and could not be identified. I can only hope that By had to go on with the teams and could not send me word, and he thinks *I* am well cared for, with Sam and Dora.

Sunday, July 22nd

Judge Holly came from the mountains today and brings me tidings of By. He had gone to the mountains sure enough. So I am relieved. He will be home tomorrow. I am thankful. Yes, I have many blessings, and a feeling of gratitude to my Heavenly Father fills my heart. I have been out on the prairie and gathered a lovely bouquet of flowers. I sent a bundle of letters home today by Cousin Tom Wymond.

Monday

This has been a day of horrors. There has been four men killed in saloons. There is talk of a vigilance committee. There is too much lawlessness going on, so many saloons and dens of vice. I have been acting sister of charity for a few days. A poor old lady is very sick in a tent back of the house. I have watched two nights there. I cook her breakfast and carry it over every morning. My hens keep me supplied with eggs. I exchange them for meat and vegetables or milk at the rate of $2.00 per dozen. I have traded sewing for a fine brahma rooster—$5.00 I paid for him. Also bought a nice large looking glass, some tubs, and lots of little things. The currency here is mostly in gold dust, or small nuggets. It is carried around in small bottles or buckskin bags, and weighed out on small scales. You cannot get less than 25 cents worth of hardly anything. People don't seem to value money, at least those who are making it, since some of them make it so easily. I get fabulous prices for sewing.

Tuesday, July 24th

I had three young girls to spend the day. We were quite hilarious, for Sallie Chivington is a case to act up. Two men came to the door and pretended to want to rent the house, as there was a sign "To Rent," and I, the only agent, I asked them in, and innocently mentioned about my husband being gone. In the evening one of them came back, and not until then did I realize that I had been indiscreet. He started to come in, without invitation, with a greeting that almost paralyzed me. I screamed to Mr. Van Tell across the street, raised the broomstick that I was using to bring down on his worthless head, when he turned and fled. It all came over me how unprotected I was, so far from home and friends, and with perhaps too little knowledge of the world. I threw myself upon the floor and cried and cried until I was sick.

Wednesday, July 25th

My darling came home today. He was shocked and distressed to think how I had been situated during his absence. He wrote me a letter two days after leaving, telling of his changed plans, that was never delivered to me. We are to go to the mountains. On Saturday the teams will be here, so I shall be more than busy.

Gold Hill,* Rocky Mountains

We left Denver Sat. 28th, afternoon. Travelled 4 miles and camped. Reached Boulder Sunday afternoon, a distance of 30 miles. Our road was very rough, full of boulders. Here there is an extensive valley and some farms, fenced in. Boulder is composed of perhaps a dozen cabins.

* Gold Hill was a small mining camp northwest of Boulder. The Gold Hill Mining District was created on March 17, 1859, and its regulations served as guide for much subsequent mining law.

Boulder Creek is a fast rushing stream, clear as crystal, and full of small trout. Under the shadow of immense mountains this little spot is sheltered, a picturesque place for habitation. On Monday morning we began ascending the mountains. We would go up such steep places that I thought the wagon would fall back on me. I would yell to get out, but found my breath too short to climb far. Our driver assured me the cattle were sure-footed and it was safer to ride, so I would climb back and rest. But I could but be charmed with the surroundings. The rocks are grand! the hills covered with evergreens of spruce and pine, flowers are growing everywhere, peeping here and there from the crevices of the rocks, bright cold springs start out here and there, and silvery cascades come leaping down the mountainsides. Altho we seemed so high, there were peaks that rose hundreds of feet above us. There are a number of cabins on Gold Hill occupied by miners, the largest owned by Holly and Holt, who are putting up a stamp mill. We are in the gulch below, where McKnight is putting up his mill. By is to do the blacksmithing for the company, and as was arranged I am to cook for the men. My heart sinks within me when I see there are 18 or 20, and no conveniences at all. There is a rough log cabin, neither chinked nor daubed, as they call it, no floor, and only a hole cut out for a door and window. A "bunk" is made in one corner. This is covered with pine boughs, and on this are spread our comforts and blankets. We have no mattress—can't even get straw or hay to fill a bed tick. I have to cook out of doors by a fire, but have mustered my small cook stove into service, but that will only hold one loaf of bread, or one pie at a time. All I have furnished to cook is bread, meat, and coffee. The cups and plates are of tin. A long table is made in a shed made of the pine boughs outside the cabin. No table linen is supplied. I fear I shall sink under this burden. It is not what my fancy painted it.

By has been helping me until I get started, but he does all sorts of awkward things. If this does not take the romance out of me, then I'm proof against *anything*. McKnight is a rough sort of man and don't seem to know that a woman needs more to do with than men. Mr. Holly comes down to see us often and looks as if he pitied me. There are some very nice boys here. They are nice to me in every way. They sing of evenings and that helps while the time away. They sang "Home Sweet Home" last night and I softly cried myself to sleep.

August 7th, Sabbath evening

I snatch a moment to write tonight. The week has been spent in monotonous routine. Cook, cook, bake, bake! The fire to cook by is built in a pile of rocks. They get so hot that it almost burns my face to a blister. The boys voted they would get their own dinner today, so Judge Holly, By, and I took a long walk up where we had a lovely view of the snowy range, and also of the plains, that stretched out like a map. We can see Denver 40 miles away. Called at a cabin and had a sight of a new little baby a week old. I should call her "Treasure" if she were mine. There are only 5 ladies on this Hill.

Tuesday, 9th

Have just arisen from my couch of fragrant pine leaves. That *is* one luxury, the perfume of the evergreens. I have been sick two days. By will not allow me to stay here, and has given up his place, so we are about to be thrown out on the cold charity of the world. Mr. Holly has invited us to come up to their cabin until I get better, and says, "Never fret. There will be something 'turn up.'" Jim Bond was here today. He said, "Why! Mollie, you can't stand this."

Friday

We left our prison in the gulch. Are at the Holly and Holt house on the hill. They have 3 or 4 cabins together, and things look homelike, dirt floors as all have, but glass windows and doors and have a large cooking stove.

I have been quite sick. The lady who does the cooking here is a dear little body and has taken care of me. Dr. Holt pulled a large tooth for me today, and now I hope to be better. When we first came to Denver, By put his horses on a ranch near there. The first night one of them broke its neck on the lariat rope. He has traded the other for an Eraster Wheel,* some sort of contrivance to be run by water power to grind the rocks to get the gold. He is off now working it. It seems too uncertain for *me* to have any faith in. I am in a room alone, and believe I feel more sad and homesick than ever before in my life.

Mrs. Lochman has just been in and said, "Dear me! You look as if you hadn't a friend in the world. Cheer up, everyone else is in good spirits, and Mr. Sanford is going to make his fortune at that wheel." I know I have a friend, One who never deserts those that trust Him.

I believe one reason of my homesickness is that I do not hear from home. They must have written, but our mails come every way, or *any* way. "Little Book!" do you think I'm naughty? *Do* you suppose I'm morbid? I have a horror of either.

Saturday, August 15th

It is now the middle of August and very cold. We have had a fire all day. I wrote letters all the morning. We are boarding now, so I have very little to do. I assist Mrs. Lochman occasionally. I am feeling better again. By took

* The "Eraster Wheel" was an *arrastre*, an old Spanish mining device for crushing ore by means of a drag stone.

me down in the gulch to see his Eraster wheel. I saw the "wheel," but have failed to see any gold that it has ground out yet, but By is very sanguine. We climbed a high mountain. The grandeur of these mountains is deeply impressive. They seem of endless extent. We could look down into the gulches and see where several mills are in operation, stamping and grinding the precious ores that are dug from the bowels of those hills. The shrill steam whistles would come reverberating and echoing over the hills, making it seem that there is some enterprise somewhere. The Holly and Holt mill is not in operation yet.

Sunday, 16th

A day of rest from the labor of the week. Bright and glorious it dawned. Divine service was held on the hill today, in one of the empty cabins. The preacher was a white-haired veteran of the cross. He spoke of the miners, delving into these hills to reach their precious treasures, and bade them not forget to lay up treasures that fade not away. Mrs. Lochman and husband are going to leave here, to return to their home in the east, and I will probably take her place. I believe I can manage the house here, as there are many more conveniences, and I can have more help.

Thursday

The Lochmans have left, and I am installed as housekeeper. There are 20 men to cook for, but so far I have got along splendidly. Mr. Holly is a kind friend, and when By gets tired of his wheel, will give him employment. There are two young ladies with their two brothers living next door to us. They are so much company for me. Had a letter from Dora. She is happy and they are doing well.

Sunday eve

Another comes. Thus it is time keeps moving on in

ceaseless steady motion. I *do* take a little time now and then, amid all my work, to moralize. I will not put myself down to ceaseless drudgery. I must *think* and *read* and do something, so that I shall at least not retrograde. 'Tis a glorious Indian summer day; over the mountains and plains hangs a soft hazy mist that gives everything a calm, subdued effect. Soft breezes are wafted into my cabin door. I love everything and everybody today. I look upon these beauteous surroundings and bless the hand that made them. I have been roaming in fancy today, in the lovely fields and woods of my sweet "Hazel Dell." I can see the sparkling "Nemaha" and my little brothers sporting on its grassy banks, and hear the voices of the older one anon, speaking of the absent ones. My sweet *sweet* home! Why did I *ever* leave you in the strangers' land to dwell? Down deep in my heart I feel that irrepressible yearning to be once more within your portals. A copy of the Neb. City News came today, with the notice of sister Anna's marriage to Mr. Harvey. She had been in town, I heard, with Mrs. Dr. Rankin, and the match was made. I have had no recent letters, and it does seem too bad. I'm sure it would cure this homesickness to get a good letter. "Holly and Holt" are having trouble with their mill, for the want of water. By and Judge went to Boulder today. Our mail comes there and has to be brought up here by anyone coming. I did not want By to go today. He is away all the week at his "wheel," and I see so little of him. By the time he climbs the hill of nights he is too tired to keep awake. I feel that—

> It was for him I left my happy home.
> With him 'mid all life's cares to roam.
> To him I gave my maiden heart,
> And bade all other loves depart.

*   *   *   *

O! my husband, how I love him,
Every look, and every word,
When I think of sweet emotions
His dear looks and words have stirred;

Looks that told me I was dearer—
Than all else on earth beside,
Words that blest me with their sweetness
While I lingered by his side.

How these memories warm my lone heart
On this quiet afternoon—
Making blossoms in my pathway
Shed their incense of perfume.

Making sunshine of the shadows—
Making gladness of the gloom.
Yes, they make me very happy
On this lovely afternoon.

Now, if By were to see this, he would make sport of me, but he never looks into this Journal, I'm sure. I was up at Mrs. McCanlin's, my nearest neighbor on the other side. She has a lovely baby girl. I go to see the baby, for Mrs. Mc., she is so quiet, you can hardly get her to converse at all. I believe she is afraid of her husband. He seems cross and sullen.

Friday, September 28th

A cold, dreary day. The boys are congregated around the stove, poor fellows! They are all away from home. No doubt they feel homesick too. They are all so kind to me. By and Judge saw Mr. and Mrs. Decker while at Boulder. A number of Nebraska people are there. I have worked very hard today. The item of bread alone is something *awful* to keep up. We do not have much of a variety. Our hens, with some belonging to the company, keep us in eggs, and we have the milk from two cows. I had a visit from two little boys today. I hugged them and kissed them for the little brothers far away. I feel stiff and lame tonight. Have raised my eyes to look into the glass. I see that Mollie Sanford does not look as fair as Mollie Dorsey did one year ago. Mountain air has given her a browner tinge.

October 5th

The month of October again. Time does pass more quickly than I thought it could. Have a letter from Dora. They have moved to Denver. She needs me so much, but I am unable to go to her now. Several families left the Hill today. They do not want to winter here. I half wish I were going too. I do not feel entirely amiable today. My heart has been like a turbulent stream, whose waters rush on in querulous motion. My little bark dashes out on the turbid waves today. It should have been moored in a quiet harbor. I sit listlessly with dripping oars, and heed not its wayward direction. Over the dark river I see the green shores and bright sunshine I can behold but not reach! Must I thus recklessly dash along without one effort to make the brighter side? Must I remain in the shadow when I might reach the sunshine? Rouse, faint heart. Does not everything of beauty beckon me ashore?

There! my effort has saved me. I leave the troubled waters behind. I am so full of moods. I know how wrong and useless it is to feel blue. Well for me it is, my good angel lifts me out of these momentary fits of despondency. I guess I get too tired, or too something. Why don't I hear from home?

Sunday, October 14

I had a good cry today because everyone else had

letters but myself. Some of the boys are going to Boulder. I thought I would write once more. I went outside the cabin door, by *my* big "rock." From there I could see the plains stretching eastward as far as the eye could reach. I wished myself a fairy or spirit, that I might fly away to the old home and see them all once more, and soon I transferred my longing to paper—*Dear friends,* I said,

I'll come upon this glorious day
In spirit form and visit you.
I'll soar o'er mountains, hill, and plain
To be with you at Hazel Dell again.

In spirit form I'll take my flight,
My starting place shall be yon mountain's height;
From that tall peak—that seems to touch the sky
I'll start upon my voyage—I will fly

Swift as some uncaged bird set free,
Over the mountain, over the lea,
On through the heaven's misty dome
Back to my girlhood's happy home.

* * * * *

You look amazed to see my face,
Sweet wonder in your eyes I trace,
I come on fairy wings today
From mountain peaks so far away.

It is pretty hard to come down from the realms of fairies, to the *degrading* position of cook, but such is my fate, and I suppose these hungry men appreciate my cooking more than they would my verses. I suppose I ought to stick to the one or the other as I cannot make a success of either.

This afternoon I took a walk alone. By had gone away with the boys. I found a large rock that hung over the side of the hill, which made a secure shelter. Into this I crept, and thought, and thought, and *wept*, for what? I *suppose* because I was alone, and homesick. I could see nothing but frowning rocks, and watch the falling leaves of the poplars. Then I prayed a while, and felt better. As I came home I gathered the crimson and yellow leaves and mingled with them some juniper berries and evergreens. This taught me a lesson of life. The falling leaves were death, the evergreens, life everlasting. I came to the cabin and gave the boys their supper and then went in to see the girls, but they have their young gentlemen friends of Sunday evenings. So I came to my journal, and now it is time to stop. I must to bed to rest for the labors of another day.

October 20th

Eliza Noel, the older of the girls next door, has been helping me today. She said, "Now, Mrs. Sanford, if you will write me a letter and some nice verses, I'll make you a kettle of soft-soap." As the writing was more to my taste, I made the exchange, but fear she got the worst of the bargain. It seems Eliza has about raised her brothers and sister, as they were left orphans. She has no education, but she is thoroughly *good*, and *appears* quite well. Mr. Holly read to us a while. He is very kind, and helps lighten my labors.

October 22nd

I have put away my work, and taken up my pen, hardly knowing what to write or to say.

Judge Holly went to Boulder today and perhaps I'll get a letter. I am ashamed to be so homesick. Of course I do not *say* all that I inscribe here. This is my "confidante." I try to be cheerful for By's sake, for fear he might think I wasn't happy with him. He hasn't the family ties that I have and cannot understand. He has no own brothers or sisters living, and that makes a difference.

October 23rd

Yes! dear little book, I have had a letter, a whole bunch of them. The dear ones have written. They have been sent to California, some of them. They are full of love and sympathy, and I will be happier. Besides, I am going to Denver to visit Dora for a few days. This is Ada's birthday. She is now in her "teens," is a comfort to Mother. The weather is cold. By has left his frozen-up "wheel" and gone to work for Holly and Holt. The man that got his horse has the best of the trade. By seems infatuated with the prospecting and working of ores.*

November 10th

Denver, and so much improved, I hardly know the place. Dora looks so well, and has her shanty looking cozy and nice. We are so happy together, but our time is brief. Mrs. Decker came down with me in the coach. Is stopping with a friend. There is a deep snow on the ground and no going around much, altho I have been to the dry goods store and made some purchases. The prices frighten me, so I had to be very careful.

On Monday there was a jubilee over the recent Presidential election. The Republicans gained the victory, and *Abraham Lincoln* is the President of these United States. The people cannot vote in the Territory, but they can demonstrate their feelings. Judge Bennet was the orator of the day, and being one of our old Nebraska townsmen, we feel justly proud. I find Dora's neighbors very sociable and

* By's biographies state that he had one of the first stamp mills in Boulder County and that "his knowledge of metallurgy and love for the mountains led him into several mining ventures. He discovered the first tellarium brought to light in the Rocky Mountain region" (Denver *Post*, November 27, 1914).

pleasant. Could I have such associations I would not get so lonely.

"Gold Hill"—November 30th [?]

"Home again," and the little cabin looks good to me, and By looks *sweeter* than ever. We had a horrid trip in the coach coming from Denver. I almost froze my feet. Mr. Holly went and came back as I did. I stopped with Mrs. Decker overnight in Boulder and came up the mountain in an ox team. We came thro drifts 4 feet deep. Eliza Noel cooked while I was gone. The boys are glad to have their old cook back again. Our stock of provision is fast disappearing, and I fear we shall see harder times. Mr. Holly got a few bushels of potatoes, the first we have had. They are no larger than a good-sized walnut. We count them luxuries. I use them in soup, and have fried potatoes of Sundays for breakfast. We have dug a hole in the floor of the eating room and buried them, as we have no cellar. The company has been unfortunate in putting their mill up here. They cannot get sufficient water. They are moving it to Left Hand Creek.

December 5th

The weather is severe, the snow piled up in heavy drifts. The girls left yesterday for California. I shall miss Eliza. She was like a mother to me. We are going into a small cabin by ourselves. I cannot do the work any longer. Beside, I did not get any money for it. The company haven't it. We turned in our provision when we came, so we have that refunded, and will not suffer. The company's stores have been mysteriously disappearing, and our potatoes that were so precious one morning were found entirely gone. We did not know whom to accuse, as there are no families but one here. The men employed get their board, and no one could account for the disappearance. We have a wagon sheet stretched across over the table to keep the dirt falling from the roof. I noticed it hanging down as if full of dirt. I had By take it down, and there, frozen as hard as bullets, were our little potatoes, carried there by the mountain rats. This led to a further investigation, and behind the lining of clapboards of the provision room we found stowed away candles, bars of soap, dried apples, and crackers that the mischievous creatures had put there. These rats have bushy tails and are a species of ground squirrel. It is almost incredible the amount they can carry. I am feeling better since my trip to Denver. I will stay here until the first of the year. My new cabin will be done.

December 17th

This is my 22nd birthday, bright and beautiful. Thus the years come and go. Still my life is spared, and "goodness and mercy still follows me."

My only present was a writing desk and gold pen and case from Mr. Holly, very pretty and very acceptable. My darling kissed me 20 times 22. I get frequent letters from home. The verses were highly appreciated. Mother writes the whole family cried as Father in trembling tones read them. I shall probably never feel as homesick again. Little Journal, *aren't you glad?*

Christmas, December 25th

We tried to have a good time, but had to make our dinners on meat, bread, and dried apple pie. But for those pesky rats we might have had potatoes. They certainly would be considered a luxury at 12 ½ cents per pound. The men folks are all discouraged. They came here expecting to pick up the gold almost on the surface of the ground, but they find it takes hard work and more money to dig the gold out of these hills. Some of the rougher element were drunk today, but there are some fine young fellows among them.

How are they at home today and do they miss me much?

My Christmas present was a flask of whisky some of the boys had left. Patrick, a good-natured Irishman, brought it, saying, "It's thinkin' we did that ye might nade it in case of sickness, or snakebite, ye know." A lecture on temperance would have been just then like "casting pearls before swine," so I took the flask, and resolving no one else should feel the effects of it, filled it with camphor gum to be sure it should be used in "case of sickness." By came in a little chilled this eve and thought he would "just taste it." When it almost strangled him, he then gave *me* a lecture for being *too* much temperance, which is by no means "casting pearls."

CHAPTER EIGHT

Gold Hill, Left Hand Creek, Denver, and Fort Lyon

January 1, 1861–February 28, 1862

New Year's, January 1st, 1861

Finds me duly domiciled in my little cabin. I have it arranged real nicely. One of the boys made a fancy top bedstead out of some white pine boards, pieces of a packing box. I took some brick dust that I had been provided with for scouring purposes, and mixing with linseed oil, stained it so that it looks like light cherry. I have an oiled wagon cover on my ground floor, white curtains to my little window of three panes of glass, my cook stove, and some stools. Have made a rocker out of a barrel, and covered and cushioned it. We have a large fireplace, and pile the pine logs on and really I feel as if I am in a palace now. I enjoy getting our meals. Mr. Holly eats with us most of the time. I feel sorry for him. He has lost so much money. He is just as kind to us as he can be. I have had a present of Scott's novels in nice binding. I read a great deal, and am doing up some necessary sewing.

January 10th

By is gone on a business trip for the company. Will be in Denver a day to see Sam and Dora. I miss him of nights. I have a little 12-year-old girl staying with me.

January 25th

Have news from Dora. She has a baby boy. They call him Frank, and now I shall not rest until I see the little fellow. By says he is pretty. By returned all right and has to go back again soon. I have *actually* been invited out to tea. A family are living in the gulch below a couple of miles, of whose existence I was ignorant until a few days ago. They called upon me. Mrs. Glotfetter is a good motherly woman, has a sweet little girl. The people here are discouraged because the mines do not turn out as well as in other districts. By went to see other mills to get some ideas about the saving of the gold. He is determined to stick to Holly and Holt until they make or break.

February 10th

And By gone again, this time to "Gregory." * I have not written much of late. We had a scare today. The news was brought in that Indians were on the warpath and would probably attack the mining towns! My cabin stands off alone, so I did not care to stay alone and be butchered. Went to Mrs. Glotfetter's where we could all be slaughtered together. The men gathered all the firearms and congregated in an empty cabin. We had arranged if the worst came to the worst, we would get in the buckets and be let down some of the mining shafts, let down by a windlass, but I said, "No, let *me* die the death of the brave." I knew if we women were stowed away in the bowels of the earth, and

* Gregory was named for John H. Gregory who in May, 1859 made one of the most celebrated gold strikes in Colorado.

all the men killed, who would rescue us? I would as soon be scalped as buried alive! After a night of suspense, we were informed that it was a hoax. The perpetrator of the joke could not be found or I think there would have been some hair lost, but not by scalping.

We had a call from Mr. W. N. Byers,* editor of the Rocky Mountain News. Mr. Holly paraded some of my verses and Mr. Byers has solicited contributions, has given me a six-month subscription to his valuable paper. A poor fellow was buried on the Hill today. He was off in a cabin alone, and had been sick for days. When found was too far gone to be helped. He has a young wife back east. I do not feel safe to have By tramping over these lonely mountains alone. Tonight I feel homesick and lonesome.

February 14th

Surely must I pen a few lines on this the first anniversary of my marriage. I felt so sorry to have By away. I looked for him all day, but when darkness settled down upon the mountains I gave up his coming. I prepared a nice supper, or as good as I could. I put on my whitest tablecloth, and had the brightest of fires. Little Jennie Glotfetter is with me, but by 9 o'clock she was asleep. I sat gazing into the blazing fire, thinking how one year ago tonight I was an anxious waiting bride, and something seemed to tell me he would come, improbable as it seemed. But I kept the kettle singing on the stove, the logs piled on the fire, and every few moments would peer out into the midnight darkness to catch the sound of his coming. At last I heard a noise, a step on the threshold! and By was at home. He had

* William N. Byers was another former Nebraskan who played a considerable part in early Colorado. Born in Ohio, he had lived in Iowa and settled in Omaha in 1854. He had served in Nebraska Territory as a member of the first legislature and as deputy surveyor. In 1859 he came to Denver, where he established the *Rocky Mountain News.*

walked 10 miles over that lonely road just to be with me on our first anniversary, and if *any*one, or if *I* myself, ever thought him devoid of sentiment, *that* decides that he is not. He is lying on the bed resting, and I so happy I had to tell my Journal.

March 12th

By came in this morning with the news that we had to move down in the Left Hand Gulch where Holly and Holt mill is located. Just as I was becoming attached to my little cute cabin home. The "Hill" will be deserted, so I suppose there is nothing to do but up and follow the company.

March 15th—"Left Hand Creek"

It comes rushing down the canyon, over the huge boulders like a torrent. Steep high mountains are on either side. It would be pretty here, but a recent fire has swept over the place, blackening the trees. We do not get the benefit of the sun until 9 o'clock in the morning, and lose sight of it about 4 P.M. Our cabin is below the mill a couple of hundred yards and the last one for miles. The distance from the "Hill" is three miles. I walked, as the road is so steep, and found my level several times on the icy ground. O! dear me! There's no use in trying to see much romance in this wild life. My cabin is made of black logs. There is a doorway but no door, not even a *hole* for a window. All the light I have when it is cold is what comes in around the stovepipe where the hole is too large. A blanket is hung up to the door, a rock tied on the ends to keep it down.

O! come balmy spring, so that my door may always be open. I am to spend the summer in Denver, and By is to build us a good house. Perhaps when I come back I may bring something to brighten and cheer our home for many years. I have letters from Dora urging me to come at once, but I cannot leave By any longer than necessary.

April 15th

I am still alive, and have been here a whole month! The weather now is lovely and I spend my time rambling up and down the creek, and tending my chickens. I have a brood of little chicks. By is making a little garden on a small plot across from the cabin, and I am quite content. I have a neighbor, a Mrs. Breach, who cooks for a mill company in the gulch. She has been to see me once, and think I shall like her. The mill is in operation now, and they are getting some return for their labor. By works on the night shift, and I'm alone until midnight. Mr. Holly often comes in and reads until 9 o'clock. I am reading a good deal. I have a work by Robert Dale Owens, "Footprints on the Boundaries of Another World," full of marvelous and supernatural. I read last night very late, and instead of it making me nervous, I actually wished I might see something to convince me. I often read until weary, then blow my candle out, and say, "Now come on, ye apparitions." One night after having made this tragic demand, and awaiting an "evidence," I heard a noise like the faint cry of an infant. I had not calculated on a speaking witness, and for a moment my brave heart quailed. Again I heard the sound nearer, and nearer, then a scratching at the blanket, then the sound like the mewing of a cat. I struck a match and lighted my candle, and there in the middle of the floor stood a little white kitten! I scarcely breathed, and thought, "Do spirits ever come in feline form?" I determined to ascertain, and uttered in a dramatic voice, "If you are a spirit, depart, if a kitten, come to me!" At the sound of my voice, the little creature leaped upon the bed, and came purring around my neck in a very material fashion. I took it as a gift from fairyland, for there are no cats or kittens in these mountains.

But the next day Mrs. Breach came in and, seeing it, exclaimed, "O! there's my pet. Where did *you* get my kitten?" So I had to lose *it*, as well as the little faith I had in "manifestations."

Mr. Decker called today. He was once a good Methodist, and my class leader. He is now, they say, drifting into Spiritualism. I seem to have lost my faculty to foresee events and am glad of it! Don't want to be a "witch."

May 10th

I am about to go to Denver. I dread to leave By and my black log cabin, for I have been very happy here, never have had a homesick day hardly. I guess the altitude and the hard work was too much for my nerves on the hill. My health is perfect, and only circumstances make me leave the place now. R'vnd John Chivington is here locating a Masonic Lodge. By will take the first degree. He takes charge of me to Denver. We go by team to Boulder, where I stop overnight with Mrs. Decker, and then go by coach to Denver. I have packed my belongings, and By will board at the mill.

May 20th

I arrived all right in Denver last eve. I had a narrow escape from being killed. Just as I said good-by to my husband, the team started up suddenly. The seat on the wagon, the *back* seat, was loose, and over it went with me. I thought I was killed, but after resting a while I started on. That night at Mrs. Decker's I was very ill, and had a physician, but he gave me remedies that helped me, and yesterday I came down. Dora and Frank are well, and so glad to see me, but I find I must look for some boarding place, as her room is so small, now that the baby has come, but I will be somewhere near her.

June 1st

Finds me at my new boarding place 8 miles up the Platte, at the home of Mrs. Woodrow. They have a small house, and four children, but the days are fine and we almost live out of doors. The children sleep in a tent. We are in a perfect wilderness of wild roses and vines with great forest trees and wild fruit, so I am in my element. Were By only here I would be perfectly happy. Dora can come up often to see me. I like the family. Mrs. Woodrow is certainly the most congenial person I have met. Mr. Woodrow is easy-going and good-natured, hardly equal, I should think, to his wife in intellect, but they are a happy family.

We had company today, Mr. John McBroom, bachelor, and his sister-in-law, Mrs. Emma McBroom. She is a dear little woman, with a perfect cherub of a child, sweet-faced Eva, an only child. It is wonderful how people do dispose of their company with their meagre accommodations, but they do, and everyone has good times. There can't be much jealousy, for one is not much better off than others, so there is a feeling of brotherhood with all. We had a nice dinner, and then visited out under the trees, while the children skipped pebbles over the water. The Platte River runs through this place. The days are hot, but the nights are cool. The evening breezes come down from the hills, and light showers fall every afternoon. I never tire of the landscape. Each morning I see some new lights and shadows, something I had not seen before. I often look toward the north, where Long's Peak looms up white-capped and grand, and think almost beneath its shadows is my mountain home and my loved one, and I sigh for the music of the cascade and the companionship of my husband. He will be with me sometime this summer.

August 20th

Of course I am happy now, for By is here. This is the happiest family I have seen since I left my home in Neb., and yet the parents are not mated. There seems to be so much sympathy between the parents and children, especially with the mother. They simply worship her, and everyone loves her. I feel so fortunate to have secured so good a place and kind a friend during my exile from home. By has our house about done, and we anticipate much pleasure when we go home. I know I shall never be so homesick again. I have heard that the first year of married life was a severe trial, the getting weaned from home, and the adapting of dispositions.

September 25th

After many weeks I again seek my Journal. On the 28th of August my little babe was born, a beautiful boy, but he did not stay with us. God took him to his fold, this one pet lamb. When I first looked on his little face, he was in his little coffin, dressed in one of the sweetest of the robes I had made, into whose stitches I had woven dreams of my angel baby. This was my first great grief. By was not permitted to look upon his "first born." He had gone away for a few days, expecting to return soon. When he next heard of me, it was that I was dying. He hurried to my bedside, for days nursing me with the tenderest care. We dare not murmur at our loss, altho a great disappointment, for *my* life was spared. As soon as I was able I came to Dora, where I now am. By has returned to the mountains.

I left the Woodrows with regret. Mrs. W. had taken excellent care of me, and I loved them all.

The town is now in a fever of excitement. There is war and rumors of war. Troops are being organized, Gov. Gilpin calling for volunteers. The South has seceded and our country is to be plunged into civil war. By writes me that he can have the appointment of 2nd lieut. in the 1st Colorado Regiment* now being raised here, and says, "Shall I accept?" I can hardly say. I know thousands of men are leaving homes and families to go. The troops, they say, will not leave Colo., and perhaps not Denver. A military post is to be established. R'vnd Chivington has the commission of Maj. It may be for the best for By to accept this position. The company in the mountains have entirely broken up, and we can hardly go back there. He will be here again soon. I am not able to be around much, but do enjoy these lovely days.

October 5th

By is down again. He has received his commission as 2nd Lieut. of Company H, Colorado Volunteers. He will leave soon to go on a recruiting trip through the mountains. Denver is a busy place. I never thought to be the wife of a soldier. I have heard war predicted by sage prophets. It has been coming on for years, but I hardly realized the issue would come in my time.

October 10th

All is bustle and confusion. Bands are parading the streets. The sound of fife and drum is heard from morn till night. By is at Central City. They do not have to drum up the recruits, they come in from all quarters, from the mines, the shops and stores, all ready to fight for their country. Several of the Gold Hill boys have gone into By's company.

I have had an invitation to attend a Regimental Ball given

* The First Regiment of Colorado Volunteer Infantry was raised in the summer and autumn of 1861, and Camp Weld was established on the east bank of the South Platte River about two miles south of the center of Denver.

by the Governor to the Officers. It comes from Hon. C. M. Chilcott.* Mr. Holly introduced him to me. I care nothing about going as I do not dance, neither does Mr. Chilcott, as he has rheumatism. Sam and Dora insist on my going. I have gotten out my wedding dress, and by some alterations will make it do. As a spectator I do not need to be particular. I only go to represent By.

October 18th

No! I did not go to the "Ball." The night that I should have been there, mixing with the wealth and beauty of this metropolis, the observed of all observers, I was piled up in bed, with a swollen jaw, my face decorated with a poultice.

I did not care much, as I would rather not have gone with a stranger.

We had letters from home today, not very encouraging. Crops have failed, and very hard times are in store for them, I fear. We got up a box of little things and sent to them. My little baby's clothes I sent to Anna. She and Mr. Harvey are at home with the folks.

November 1st

And we are settled at the barracks. I have a good room and some furniture, but bare floor. This is better than the ground, however. We have a cook. By had been telling about their queer little French cook "Henry." When I met him he bowed and held out his hand, stammering, "Nebraska Ceety, de fine young ladee, de school, de bouquet," and all at once I recognized the dapper little Frenchman that gave me the bouquet, but he had changed from

* George M. Chilcott came to Colorado from Burt County, Nebraska, in 1859. He was a member of the first two sessions of the Colorado legislature. He later served as United States Senator from Colorado.

his fine suit into the garb of cook, from a stovepipe hat to his paper skull cap, but I am sure of willing servitude. He told Capt. Sanborn * he would "die for *de Missus*." I would rather he show his devotion by living and waiting on me. The Officers in our company are Capt. Sanborn and 1st Lieut. Bonesteel. We comprise one family. We have a full regiment of soldiers, and all the retinue of a military camp, with the pomp and ceremony, and not the realities of war. Scouting parties are sent out to look after hostile Indians. There are companies drilling constantly, as both Officers and men are mostly new recruits. I find some nice families. Capt. Sopris of Co. A has a nice family, two young ladies.** The first night I was here I was alone, By having gone to Golden City. I had a dreadful toothache, and was almost frantic. Our rooms here are only divided from our neighbors' by board partitions. My groans attracted the attention of the "Orderly's" wife, who occupies the adjoining room. She came to the door about midnight and asked to come in, made a big fire in our fireplace, and soon had a steaming poultice applied, then crept in bed with me and stayed until morning. She is also a Mrs. Sanford.

We hear of fighting in the east, and of some depredations by Indians on the unprotected settlers on the plains. No more for a while can our land be called one of "peace and plenty." We hope and pray these things may soon be settled.

November 10th

It *is* a comfort to be where I can see my sister every day, for not a day passes but I go up in some of the wagons or ambulances to town. The barracks are one and a half miles below. My health is not good, and I keep outdoors as much as I can. Sam Harris and By have gone on a trip to look at some land south of Denver. Dora and I stay with

---

* George L. Sanborn was captain of Company H.
** Richard Sopris was captain of Company C.

each other alternately. Little Frank is delighted with the music of the band, and the horses. We attended service at the hospital today. The chaplain is a white-haired patriarch. I came across a cousin I had not seen since childhood at the hospital today. Happened to hear him called by the name of Wymond, and at once ascertained his pedigree.

November 15th

The boys have returned and are delighted with the country south of the Divide. We have had some sad news from home. Our dear little brother Charlie died of diphtheria on the 5th of this month. This is a terrible affliction. He was the household treasure, but, my little brother, you have gone to brighter fields and fairer shores. The Good Shepherd has called you to His fold and no harm can ever come to you. But it is hard to see you go. God pity my poor parents in this affliction. My Grandfather died in June after a short illness and "little brother" was taken to Nebraska City and buried by his side.

December 20th

Today two companies, "H" and "G" of the regiment, were ordered to garrison Fort Wise, a military post on the Arkansas River 200 miles from Denver.* The soldiers are glad of the change, but I dread going from the settlements, but this is the life of a soldier!

Dora and Sam have sold out, and are going to Iowa, to Mr. Harris' home. If he goes into the army, he prefers a home regiment where his father and brothers are fighting. It is said we will be kept at this post during the war. It is hard to change, and to travel at this season of the year, but I have no place to go, and might as well follow my hus-

* Fort Wise, later renamed Fort Lyon, was established in 1859 at the site of Bents New Fort, a fur-trading port. It was about twenty miles downstream from the present town of Fort Lyon.

band. Mrs. Sanford, or "little Mrs. Sanford" as she is called to designate her from myself, is going, and also the wives of several of the soldiers. We will not part as long as we can be together. I might go home, but in case of action and By should be wounded I would want to care for him.

There is no well-regulated hospital with sisters of mercy here. I have visited the hospital here, and often go in and read to the patients. There are about 21 of the soldiers lying there now, with snow blindness. They were out on a scout, when the sun shone down on the snow so bright. I went to all of the stores to find some dark green goods to make shades, but found none, so took my green silk parasol and made them. So I feel as if I had done something for my country. The Officers' wives are rather "tory." One of them said, "I would not be chasing after those rough men, Mrs. Sanford. Let the soldiers or laundresses look after them."

Now that war is declared, we find Denver has a great many rebel sympathizers, but let anyone advance rebel sentiments, and they do not stand much chance with the Colorado Volunteers.

I wonder to what a life I am going. I do not anticipate or speculate much. There is no use, with the varied changes that come into my life. With what little experience I have gained in mingling with different people I should be very wise and discriminating, but I find myself, with all my boasted knowledge of human nature, constantly making mistakes. I presume I am too impulsive and make friends too easily. I take it for granted that everyone is just what they pretend to be. I am commenting on this subject because I found out today that a woman whom I thought so good and pure, had run away from husband and two little children to live with one of the Officers. Such things, altho of common occurrence in this country, shock me dreadfully. I hear vague whispers about several more of the women here. One of our Gold Hill boys, Henry Renter, died at our house last week. By and I went to see him at the soldiers' quarters. He dreaded the hospital, so we brought him home, and Capt. Sanborn helped nurse him, he and the company boys, and I watched with him many hours each day, but he died, the name of "Mother" on his dying lips. He was one of the young men that had been so good to me at Gold Hill.

December 25th

I am at the Woodrows'. Sam Harris will take his team and carry our things to Ft. Lyon. Transportation is scarce. They are all ready to go east, but besides making some money, he wants to see us safely there. Dora will stay here, and so the dear sister and I part again! We have little hope of seeing each other soon again. Our paths are surely now divided, altho it is their intention after the war is over to return to this place.

Mrs. Sanford, or "Minnie," I call her, goes with me in Sam's wagon. Our marches will be slow, as it is Infantry. We have no tents and very few comforts. The soldiers get no money. Everything is paid in vouchers. Fortunately for By, he sold an interest in a lode, so that he has his dress parade suit, his sword, hat, and sash with regimental appointments and he looks handsome in his suit of blue, my soldier good and true.

January 5th, 1862

Our companies left Denver after Christmas. We had a rough trip, through an almost unsettled country. We passed thro Colorado City. There are some fine Soda Springs located in the canyon above. Several went up to see them, but I could not. I have suffered all the trip with neuralgia.

Our quarters here are pleasant, built of stone, with white

pine floors and deep large windows. The Regulars vacated when we came in. The companies that were in charge belonged to an eastern regiment and were ordered home.

Capt. Logan of Company "B" is in command, acting Major.* This is a lonely place, on a level plain, no timber in sight. The low banks of the Arkansas have a light growth of willows. There is no place to go, and few to see outside our company.

We are destitute of any kind of vegetables. Beef and whisky seem to be the staple articles. Of course we have the regulation rations, dried apples, rice, molasses, beans, and coffee. Canned fruits can be had at the sutler's store. "Henry" is still our cook, and I am indebted to his admiration of me for some little delicacies, such as snowbirds or meadowlarks broiled on toast. I have been quite sick. We had no bedstead and had to lie on the floor.

I hope the war won't be of long duration if we have to stay here. By and I went today to visit the Indian interpreter, John Smith.** He is living with a squaw. They have a little half-breed boy, called "Gov. Gilpin." They live like civilized people. I can't see how a man of Smith's abilities can live such a way.

The squaws are very fond of money and make it by selling the moccasins they make, some of which are very pretty. John wanted to be generous and make me a present, so calling By to one side he put a $5.00 gold piece in his hand, telling him to give it to Squaw Smith, who immediately on receiving it handed it over to her liege lord, with a chuckle of satisfaction. I wore my moccasins home.

* Samuel M. Logan had won attention in the first weeks of the war by tearing down a Confederate flag which had been raised over a Denver store.

** John Simpson Smith, a trader from Kentucky, was married to an Indian woman. On November 29, 1869, he was camped with Black Kettle's band at Sand Creek when Chivington attacked the village. Smith's son Jack was killed in the affair. Smith testified against Chivington in the Congressional inquiry that followed.

The boys of our company gave me a guitar. It is a "con-traband" taken from a rebel. As I have no way of returning it to the owner, I might as well play on it. Cannot play much anyway, but it does while away many a dreary hour. "Henry" is generally my audience. He said today as I sang to an accompaniment, "If Henry was in the grave and the Missus sing, Henry would come to life." If he had said it made the hair raise on his head I would believe him sooner. Of course the foolish cook keeps his place, but he doesn't get over his first enchantment at "Nebraskee Ceety."

February 14th, 1862

Two years married! We spent the afternoon in talk-ing over the old times, bringing up each reminiscence of our lives since we first met.

We have passed thro many vicissitudes and had some trials and hardships in our brief married life, but they have only cemented our hearts more closely together.

We love and live for each other. We cannot plan for the future in these troubled times. We read of dreadful battles all over, and I tremble for our country's defenders. There are fears that the Indians will become hostile. There are large bands around here all the time, coming into the Fort every day. We spent the evening at the house of the Indian Agent, Col. Boone.* He has a young wife and two grown daughters. They played cards and sipped "applejack." I took my apples without the "jack," and could not play cards. Dancing is a great source of amusement. They have frequent parties at the Fort.

February 24th

Today the Fort has been full of Indian bands that

---

* Albert Gallatin Boone, grandson of Daniel Boone, was United States Indian Agent for the Upper Arkansas River area in 1861 and was stationed at Fort Wise.

have been off somewhere else. I keep my doors locked or they would come in without ceremony. My windows are high up from the ground, but they manage to darken them with their dirty visages. I have taken my book in desperation, hoping if I pay no attention they will leave, but they keep up such a gibberish I can hardly write. One squaw has just lifted her little papoose high above the heads of the rest. It has the desired effect, for I turn my face to look at the little tously headed creature, with its tawny face and wondering eyes. One woolly pated little piccaninny at Boones and this little creature are all the "innocents" I have seen since I kissed little Frankie good-by.

There seems to be a commotion outside. Ah, I see! One of the old bucks has come, and up on the shoulders of the women he is perched, taking items from the topmost pane. He is making all sorts of gesticulations. He wants to come in, but I am impervious. Tomorrow soap and water will be in requisition, for after these visits the map of the United States is traced on my window panes.

I hear from home often. Strange, I have never been as homesick as the first year on Gold Hill. The folks want me to come home. Dora and Sam stopped and made them a visit.

February 28th

Well, I have done something I never expected to do, *played cards!* but my motive will make it all right, I hope. Our boys, Capt. Sanborn, and Lieut. Bonesteel, were constantly playing at the sutler's store and playing for cigars and, I think, wines and drinks, and sometimes By would be there. I expostulated, until finally Capt. said, "If you will learn the one game of cribbage I promise we will not go any more, but spend our evenings at home." We are still one family, so it was like keeping my own boys out of bad company, and I learned and must confess I find it fascinating for myself. Bonesteel came home intoxicated the other day, and as By was with him, I thought he was so too. By was trying to hold him up as he reeled from side to side, and they both reeled, and I cried, and O! dear me! I *was* happy when I found I was mistaken. I do believe it would break my heart to see By get in the habit of drinking. I will do all I can to keep any of them straight. They have nothing to do but kill time, and "Satan always finds work for idle hands."

I begin to feel at home here now. I have made a friend of Miss Maggie Boone, the Col.'s oldest daughter. She is quite deaf, though. That makes it a little hard to converse with her.

March 1st

I come with tearful eyes and sad heart tonight, my Journal. Yesterday I thought this was to be my home during the war, but dear me! we do not know what a day may bring forth.

The news has come by messenger that the Rebels are marching on to Fort Union on the borders of New Mexico.* The cry comes to our Regiment at Denver to come to the rescue. Our two companies are ordered to meet the regiment at Hulls Ranch on the Arkansas. Already preparations are being made to make forced marches. Poor boys! it is a long rough journey. No doubt the rebel forces outnumber ours two to one. Gen. Canby is in the field, and to his rescue are they going. Some of our brave boys are

* General Henry H. Sibley led Confederate forces in an offensive against New Mexico early in 1862. He was opposed by Federal troops under Colonel E. R. S. Canby. The Confederates, mostly Texans, captured Albuquerque and Santa Fe and advanced upon Fort Union, a Federal post northwest of Santa Fe. Colonel Canby appealed to Colorado for re-enforcements, and the First Colorado was given the assignment.

marching on to certain death. It may be my husband. God knows! The women of the company have to be sent to Denver until it is all over. I have no time to moralize.

Farewell, old Fort. May I never see you again as the wife of a soldier or until peace again reigns in our land.

CHAPTER NINE

Camp Weld, Hazel Dell, and Denver

March 8, 1862–September, 1864

Denver, March 8th

After a long siege and a long tramp I am again quartered at Camp Weld, at present my home at the house of Capt. Sopris. The second day of our journey from the Fort, By and I had to be parted. We found the regiment at Hulls Ranch. I was sick and in a bad plight. I had no money, nor no friends in Denver. Was not even as well off as the laundresses, who get their rations and a place to live. We have never had a cent in money from the government, and what little we had on hand we have exhausted. Capt. Sanborn had detailed By to go to Denver to look after some matters, but when he saw the Col. he said every man at his post, and it was not for me, sick and almost helpless, to shrink from the sacrifice. Other wives had to do the same. Other hearts were as tender, other loves as fond. I never shall forget the moment when we came to say good-by. There were a thousand men encamped around, all hurry and confusion, and no time nor place for one word in private. It came so suddenly. I felt I could hardly stand it to be left alone, worse than sick, in a strange land, so far away from friends, with a swollen face, and a breaking heart. I stood by my husband in the midst of those men, only wishing for *one* moment when I could abandon myself to grief, but I saw the tears trickling down By's cheek, and then all the heroic in my woman's nature came, and *I* turned to be the comforter. I heard a voice saying, "Trust in Me; I will that ye shall meet again."

At that moment Capt. Sopris came up and said, "Don't feel so badly. I left *my* wife." I told him briefly how I was situated, and he said, "You shall go to my home, as one of my family. I will notify my wife at once, so dry your tears and all will be well." And I have been taken in and feel at home.

There were 3 wagons carrying the women and children to Denver. The driver of the wagon that Mrs. Sanford and I occupied was a Tennesseean and we did not know, but a rebel. By had given him some private information and instructions about *me*, and I was *his* especial charge. The ride was long and rough, the weather bitter cold. The other drivers drank and caroused every night. One of the horses on our wagon died, and they had to divide up with the other teams. I had a trunk and a box of dishes, all I possessed in the world. I had to sell my dishes for almost nothing to lighten the load. Then one night we stopped at a saloon. No place else to stop. There we had a harrowing experience with some drunken rebels. Taken all together, it was the roughest experience I ever passed through, but we came out alive, and now all we are worrying about is how our soldier boys are doing. We can only get news every three or four days. Camp Weld is now occupied by the 2nd Regiment Colorado Volunteers. Mrs. Sopris boards the officers. I find a few old acquaintances, but my best friends have moved away.

I was up in Denver today and who should I meet but Mr. Pete Byram. We passed a friendly greeting. He says he is happily married. He asked me if I would like to go home, and offered me a pass on the coach to Neb. City. "Why!" he said, "Miss Mollie, I would do anything on earth for *you*." I wonder if he thought of the summer afternoon at the schoolhouse, and what might have been. I thanked Mr. Byram so cordially, but said I must be near my husband. I did feel forlorn and lonely with By so far away, and even *then* I might be a widow. Ah, Little Journal, *you* have been the recipient of many, yes *all* of my sorrows. You seem almost a part of my life.

Mrs. Sopris has some splendid boys. I always liked boys, *anyway*. I feel at home in a large family. At the Fort are a number of the absent Officers' wives. Some of them don't seem to worry but attend the dances and have jolly times. While I don't propose to mope, I don't feel like having a hilarious time until I hear how our soldier boys come out, for they are sure to have a battle, and perhaps more than one!

The Governor * took dinner at our house today. He is a bachelor, grave, but very gentlemanly. Today while he was in the room I dropped a spool of thread that rolled under the bed. He crawled halfway underneath, got the spool, bowed, and handed it to me and kept on talking with the gentlemen without noticing my thanks.

March

Today I received a letter from By, telling something of their trip, and an engagement they had had. He hasn't time to write much. The most of the news come by messengers. Their scout, or guide, Tom Pollock, has returned.

* William Gilpin was appointed Governor of Colorado by President Lincoln in 1861, arriving in Denver in May. He served until March, 1862, and lived in Denver for the remainder of his life.

He brought me from By a bottle of gold dust that one of the boys wanted him to send to me, as he could not use it. It is a loan, of course, but will enable me to get some necessary articles. Today I went up into Denver to make some purchases, paid for them from my "bottle," and marched serenely out of the store, and had gone some distance before I missed it. I rushed frantically back and only by proving a private mark did I recover it. This gave me a fright that will prevent a recurrence of my carelessness. Altho this is a gold country, it does not come without hard work. Had I lost it, I would have felt like going out to service or something desperate.

March

This exciting life, so full of suspense and expectation, is very hard on anyone. We have received news of a severe battle between the Texas Rangers and our boys at Pigeons Ranch in N. Mexico. Our men had been reinforced by Gen. Canby and marched on to meet the rebel forces. They came off victorious, but lost 5 men. This much and no more, and now we will wait 3 days before finding out who are the killed and wounded. O! I *dare* not think! Some of the women are wailing and taking on dreadfully, but I am calm and hope for the best. I find myself here, there, and everywhere, condoling with one, and cheering another, when all the time I may be the bereft one. My soldier may have fallen.*

* The Battle of Pigeons Ranch was a major victory of the campaign for the Union forces. The report of battle mentioned that Lieut. Byron N. Sanford and Capt. Lewis climbed a knoll and spiked a cannon with a steel ramrod, jammed a six-pound iron ball into the muzzle, smashed the wheels and set the ammunition on fire. In addition, the two men captured several Texans. It was stated that in the course of the exploit "the Lieutenant came dangerously near losing his life" (William Clark Whitford, *Colorado Volunteers in the Civil War. The New Mexico Campaign in 1862*, Denver: The State Historical and Natural History Society, 1906. Pp. 119-120).

[*No date*]

At last the news has come. The killed were all single men, so no widow's or orphan's wail goes up from this camp tonight, but yet, they were someone's sons and brothers.

By has written that he will soon resign and come home as soon as he can do so with honor. I need him so much. Were I well I should find something to occupy my mind so that I would not get lonesome.

I room with Irene Sopris, a sweet girl. She is so cheerful. She keeps me from getting frantic, but I cannot settle myself to do anything. I seem to be living but half a life, while in reality, I am living more than one. I trust that my child may be spared to me, that my husband may be restored to me, and pictures of a happy home come before me, when peace reigns again in our land. O! will *that* ever be?

[*No date*]

Today we have had news that a number of the 1st Regiment had resigned and were coming home, Col. Slough and Capt. Sanborn of our company. Now if our Capt. *has* resigned I fear By will not, and I am all used up. I have cried all day, and do not feel like writing. I feel like "one deserted."

[*No date*]

Last night while brooding over my troubles I had one of my impressions that By was coming home. As the names of Sanborn and Sanford often get mixed, I hoped it had this time, and sure enough! this morning the advance guard arrived, and as Col. Slough shook hands with me he said, "Let me congratulate you, Madam. You will soon see your husband." And so my dream came true, and I am happy in the anticipation of meeting him tonight. I had

[173]

a room given me today, and have been getting together a few articles, for *camping* it will be. All that we had was left at Ft. Lyon, and I presume we will never get it at all. It is real amusing to see the donations, this one and the other coming in with some article they could spare from their own scanty stores. It is a sort of gypsy life anyway here, and no one has much.

By accepting some loans, buying a few things, and some donations, I have a real home-looking place for By when he comes. He should have been here now. It is late, and I only write to fill in the time, for I cannot keep still.

[No date]

I had gone to bed last night, having given up seeing my husband. Irene was with me. As we lay there talking, among the varied footfalls on the walk I recognized his. His rap on the door settled the question, and soon I was folded in my soldier's arms, and looked upon his bronzed and bearded face.

And now our life begins again, and if we have but little of this world's goods, I feel rich!! so rich!!

[No date]

The weather is now beautiful. By has the position of Post Quartermaster. He will get the position of Forage Master after a while. At present his salary is low. He has to come down from Officer's pay to $25 per month, but this includes rations, fuel, and house rent. It does not matter. We are content. We will live, if cotton cloth is 50¢ per yard, common prints the same, and spool cotton 25¢.

I do a great many little things to help along, with my needle.

We are expecting my brother Sam. He says the folks at home are having a hard time, and he is ambitious to help himself. So By will get him employment at the Camp here.

We hear of hard-fought battles. The feeling between the North and South grows more bitter every day, but I think the Rebs more bitter, the women are, at least. While By was on the battlefield after the fight at Apache Canyon, he found a letter from a Texas sweetheart to one of the Texas Rangers where she said, "Never return to me without a necklace made of Yankees' ears."

The poor Texan was killed, and could not have carried the trophy back if he had lived, as they were completely whipped and routed by our soldiers.

Mrs. Sopris has moved to Denver and opened a large boarding house. The people are changing here all the time. My nearest neighbors now are the wives of Lieut. Soffs and Lieut. Hawley. Mrs. Soffs is my old friend and neighbor Sallie Vanpelt. Things do turn out funny.

June 26th, 1862

Brother Sam has come and has employment. He has grown to almost a man in height. The Fort here is now almost deserted. The Second Regiment have been ordered to Kansas. I spend my time, outside of my little housework, rather monotonously. I do not improve much. Where hath my muse departed? No more poetical effusions grace these pages. It is two years today since we landed in Denver. I feel almost a score of years older. Looking back over these pages, I often think if I have not changed a great deal. I certainly do not have as many funny incidents to relate as I used to have.

I do not rhapsodize so much. Am becoming more settled, I suppose. We are no better off in worldly goods, but we have had some "experiences," and I am still as hopeful that something will "turn up." I thought when By was gone if *he* were spared I would work! slave, almost starve! So if we live plainly, I won't murmur.

The summer days are lovely. Camp Weld is on the banks

of a large pond, or small lake, near a pretty grove. I often sigh for the massive oaks and green pastures of Hazel Dell. It is almost like a dream. There is something sad in the thought that we are no longer a part or parcel of the past. We naturally drift away. I might sit here and mope the hours away. No! I will not sit with folded hands. I improve every opportunity to help along. I have developed quite a business turn. When the farmers come in to sell their produce, I "barter" for it by exchanging extra rations, sacks, etc.

It might sound more in keeping with my little book to chronicle something pathetic or poetic, but this is to be a receptacle of passing events, and those that come into my life just now do not seem of the romantic. I scour my pine boards, and, looking at the clean smooth floor, I am admonished that after all I am a little better off than in 1860, when the bare ground was all the floor I could boast of.

I sing my cheerful songs, and in my heart thank kind Heaven for my accumulating blessings.

July 4th

Up in Denver they are having some sort of demonstration, but we folks here prefer to spend this sultry day lying around in the shade. O! but this is the most indolent life *I* ever led. We ladies visit alternately, gossip some. Were I to write each day's events, it would be, "Got up. Got breakfast, eat, washed dishes, got dinner, and ate again," and so on, each succeeding day the same. We might enjoy the evenings, sitting on the porch chatting, but the mosquitoes are dreadfully annoying.

November 10th

Weeks and almost months have passed since I opened this Journal. When I last inscribed my thoughts the summer days were here, the leaves and blossoms. Now they are faded and autumn's breezes blow, and the first snows of winter have come, but I come with a thankful heart. I am convalescing from a protracted illness.

I introduce to these pages my sweet baby boy, my little "Bertie." He is 6 weeks old. Born September 22nd, the day upon which Abraham Lincoln issued the Emancipation Proclamation! A marvel (I think) of loveliness. He has dark hair and large, wondering hazel eyes, and he "coos" and "crows" already. A regular little captain, already giving his orders, with no intention of having them disregarded.

Changes have occurred in the camp too. The Regiments have returned and companies of soldiers now parade the grounds. By has received his appointment as Forage Master at an increased salary.

We have been occupying the best of the quarters in the camp but have been obliged to vacate for superior officers.

I am boarding with a family nearby. Mrs. Richardson is a hard-working woman, uneducated, but *so* kind and motherly and *that* is what one needs off in a strange land. Sam has had a sick spell, and she helped nurse him back to health, and I love her for it.

December 17th

My twenty-third birthday, and this reminds me of my Journal, reminds me that I am neglecting you, little book, every day. My hands are *so* full of work, and my head so full of lullabies that I have no heart for poetry, but I *meditate* when I can. I sit and hold my boy, and dream sweet probabilities for his future, and O! my baby! may you fulfill the fruition of your mother's hopes.

My fortunes have changed again and *now* we are living in a tent. We could not get a room. Our winter is delightful and so far we find it very comfortable. It is 12 by 30 feet, two apartments, and I enjoy it. If I only had a window to look out and see something of the world.

The camp is lively and exciting. Co. "H" is back. Capt. Sanborn and Lieut. Bonesteel are frequent visitors, and Mrs. Sanford (Minnie) is living in a tent beside me. Bertie is called little "Co. H."

Born and bred as he has been in the midst of military surroundings, who knows but that he may make a great General!

January 1, 1863

The New Year has come again. To me it brings contentment. I have my husband and my baby! and a shelter. We are having very high winds and I came near not having a shelter even last night. By had gone to Denver with Bonesteel to attend the theatre. There came a terrific gust that tore my stovepipe loose from its moorings, upset my little heating stove, and set my tent on fire, but fortunately I had plenty of water, and put it out, but I burned my feet and hands. When By came home I am afraid he received a "candle lecture." We are to have some rooms as soon as they are finished off.

February 14th, 1863

Another anniversary of my marriage, and if there is anything that would call up the sentimental it should be this day. That element should not ever fade out of our lives but be kept fresh and green. I do not intend it ever shall go from me. Our lives are passing placidly along just now. We are situated in two very pleasant rooms overlooking the camp. My baby is growing sweeter every day, and I am feeling better. I have a lovely neighbor in the adjoining rooms, late from Boston, a Mrs. Bradstreet. We are near of an age, and more congenial than the most of the ladies I have met in camp. Our winter has been one of the finest I ever saw.

April 10th

I only write now when the mood seizes me. I know I am retrograding as far as any mental improvement goes, but then, I am fulfilling the duties of wife and mother. I spend more time reviewing these pages than I do in adding to them. It is pleasant pastime to live over some of the scenes and incidents here narrated. The folks at home are so anxious for me to come, but I dread the long dreary journey. The government has built a hay corral nearer Denver, of which By has charge. We are living now in the suburbs in a little two-roomed house.

The days are hot and sultry. Judge Holly's daughter Julia is stopping with us. She is very much out of health, her mind somewhat impaired, and a change to Colo. has been thought advisable. I should never have undertaken this, but for the friendship I have for her father, who has been a kind and helping friend ever since we came to the country. She is a pretty girl, and at times natural, and no one would suppose anything wrong, but she is a great responsibility and care.*

I have pleasant neighbors. My baby boy can *almost* walk alone, and we are getting along well.

November 15th [?]

The long summer has passed, with very little out of the usual routine occurring. I only come to write a line to tell you, little neglected book, that I am going *home!* Yes, back to see the dear ones once again. I leave in a few days, will go in a wagon train. It seems an undertaking to start at this season of the year, but the winters are so mild and I shall be comfortably fixed. Julia has to be taken home, and I shall go partially in charge of her. Her father is going

---

* Julia Holly, an accomplished musician, died in an Iowa institution in 1866 at the age of twenty-three.

a part of the way. Brother Sam has enlisted in the army. I will break up housekeeping and By will board with the Richardsons, and sleep in his office at the hay corral until I return.

December 26th

Hazel Dell.

> Is it me? or am I dreaming?
> Are these scenes to me but seeming?
> No! 'Tis home! I know it well,
> 'Tis my own sweet Hazel Dell.

After a tedious trip across the plains, consuming over three weeks' time, I arrived in Neb. City, where my dear Father met me. Spending the night at the Old Hamlin House, we came next day to the old home, and he who can describe or tell the feelings of a returned wanderer can know mine, as I greeted parents, brothers, and sister. All well and all here but the "Little Brother." Bertie is voted a fine baby and about takes the house. Nan is at home with *her* two little ones, so we are a numerous family. The weather all thro the trip was delightful. We did not suffer with the cold. There are ranches now every few miles, and I could not recognize the land of our former pilgrimage. Mr. Geo. Tucker was at the hotel with Father and brought us out. He is not married, but rumor has it will be soon to a sister of our neighbor and friend, Mrs. Blake. Three years of absence has made some changes. I suppose I would enjoy the outdoor surroundings more, were it the summer time, but we can visit, and we do, too. I can tell so many things of my mountain life, and this "little book" is often brought into requisition. I am to stay until spring, and By is to come for me. No danger of becoming lonely. Mother is bearing her age well. Ada has grown into a tall girl, sweet and lovable as ever. Nan looks well with *her* added cares. Mr. Harvey is on a trip somewhere, and she will be here all winter too. I do not expect to journalize much more, unless something unusual transpires.

No more *wooing widowers* to talk about.

Rumor has it my hero Alexander Mapes was accidently killed a short time ago, and "Andrew" has selected a matron to look after his poor motherless bairns, and the rest of the fellows, no one knows where *they* are. *I* only know I married the "man of my choice" and would not exchange him for a king. Letters from Dora tell of the men folks all being in the army and she living with Mr. Harris' people at Grinnell, Iowa. She is patriotism to the heart's core. She has a little daughter, "Kate."

February 14, 1863 [*1864*]

Again I chronicle the anniversary of our marriage. Just to make it seem like old times we got up a splendid dinner. While the folks do not make much money, they have an abundance of farm produce, and the boys frequently come in with 30 or 40 prairie chickens. We talked over the events of February 14, 1860, and I wrote a loving letter to By. The weather is cold. I have been to Brownville to see Uncle Chas. and the dear old Grandmother, who still survives. I was gone 5 days and left little Bert at home.

A few days ago I witnessed the death of Mother's nearest neighbor, the mother of two little children. With my own hands I prepared her for burial. O! how sad to die away from friends and home, and I could but think, but for the mercy and intervention of Providence, *someone* would have had the same to do for me. They were destitute of clothing, as so many of these poor settlers are, and when I came to dress her there seemed simply nothing I could use, but among her effects I found the remnant of her wedding dress, a fawn-colored pongee, then found her wedding bonnet, some white flowers, of course discolored, but I succeeded in fixing her up so that when her husband came in to see her, he said, "O! how did you—where did you find those things? She looks like she did when a bride." It seems to me, when we do those marvelous things, or make some wonderful transformation, there is a power behind human ingenuity and intuitions that comes from some sweet spirit, *her* guardian spirit. Who knows!

February 28th

I believe I am only to relate events of a *startling* nature, or unusual occurrence here these days. Last week one of the neighbor boys came galloping up to the door in breathless haste and informed us the "bushwackers" were almost upon us.* There had been an inoffensive old man only 6 miles away that had been murdered that morning, his house burned, and horses driven off. Father affected to treat the matter lightly, but we noticed he looked over his guns and ammunition. We had no stock to lose, as Father a few days before had sold his team, but they would probably seek plunder inside, and we decided to fortify ourselves as well as possible. As it happened, no near neighbors were at home. First we secured all the money we had, put it in a tin can, and buried it in the ash hopper in the yard. Took our best clothing, packed in a large trunk, and hid under the approach to the bridge, then supplied ourselves with all the implements of warfare on the premises, comprising axes, shovels, hatchets, and clubs. A boiler of scalding water was kept at boiling point. Each female was to battle with the weapons of defense assigned her. In case they came to

* Lawless bands of men called "bushwackers" or "jayhawkers" took advantage of the Civil War to loot under the pretense of patriotism. They were active in southeastern Nebraska during the first years of the war and were suppressed by vigorous counteraction on the part of the citizens.

close quarters, with a huge dipper Mother was to shower them with a hot bath, Nan use the ax or hatchet, and Addie the clubs, while to me was given the box of red pepper to throw into their eyes. There was no levity about these precautions. It was a matter too serious for that. About dark Father took his gun and started out to reconnoiter. We tucked the little ones safely away to sleep, and kept our sentinel at the windows. Father was out so long we feared he had met his fate. We looked and listened for the slightest sound, but all was as quiet as usual. About midnight we decided as it was such a brilliant moonlight night, they would not come, and worn out with suspense and anxiety, we went to bed, leaving Father, who chose to watch. We were just about being wooed into the security of slumber when [at] a terrific yelping and scattering of the dogs, and an exclamation of "Here they come!" from Father, we were roused, ready for action. The dogs rushed through the open door of a room that is being built in front, over Father's work bench, knocking tools and saws in every direction, and still barking and howling. Father stood with his gun, Mother near the boiler. The clubs and axes were in the hands of brave and determined women, but in vain! I searched for my box of cayenne pepper that I had placed under my pillow! Well, we waited long enough to give them a chance to attack, but soon all was quiet, but the distant barking of the dogs, that were in pursuit of *something*, and we have not found out *yet* what! Perhaps the bushwackers became disgusted at finding the barn empty, or perhaps some wild varmint was after the dogs. *We* were safe, at least, and when morning dawned, we dug up our treasures and settled down to security again. Only I spent half the morning after making my bed, in sneezing and wiping the tears from my eyes that should have afflicted the foraging bushwackers. My can had rolled down in the bed and spilled. We heard the next day that the bushwackers had not been within 20 miles of us. Still *some* stragglers may have passed our place through the night.

March 29th

By has come! and after a few days' visit we again start on a pilgrimage across those plains. He made the trip in from Colorado in less than three weeks, and we will not be over 4 going back, as he has a good team. And so it is. One jaunt after another, but I am so glad to have come, and feel that I'll never suffer so much again from homesickness.

May 2nd

Arrived in Denver without accident. The trip was very pleasant, only laid by a couple of days as Bertie had the measles. We cannot get a house at once, so are living in By's office at the corral, a board shanty. It has been raining for days. Up in the direction of the Divide the skies are as black as ink. It looks foreboding.

May—Camp Weld

On the morning of the 19th about 3 o'clock the night watchman at the corral came pounding on our door with the startling cry, "Get up. There is a flood in Cherry Creek, and hundreds of people are drowning." We could not believe but that he was fooling, until we heard the distant roar and the shouts of men like the coming of a mighty tempest. By hurriedly dressed and started away. I could not leave my sleeping boy. He came back and said I must see it. I would never probably see so awful a sight again. We bundled up Bertie and, coming over to the creek, found hundreds of people staring and shivering, some half dressed, *and* all in a state bordering on frenzy. Great inky waves rolled up 10 or 15 feet high carrying on their crests pieces and parts of houses, cattle, and for all we know human beings too. In the low places the soldiers on horseback were rescuing families, risking death to save women and children, fighting with a foe not easily vanquished. It was the chill hour of morning, hardly daylight, but huge bonfires were lighted all along the banks where drenched and half-drowned people were warmed and dried. In the confusion families were divided, and plaintive cries were heard above the roar, "O, where is my husband," or, "Where are my children," or "family."

Very little if any loss of life occurred, but homes were swept out of existence. Buildings had been erected on the sandy channel of the creek that were carried away. I came back to our shanty, got a bite of breakfast, and again we went to the scene of desolation, trying to be of some assistance. By was off on duty with the soldiers, a few only who are at Camp Weld. About 9 o'clock I heard a commotion. A man came galloping along, shouting, "All that live on the river bottoms, look out. The Platte is booming," and looking toward my shanty, I could see the water spreading like a mighty lake, and knew that all *we* had in the world was in danger, so giving "Bertie" to a trusty friend, I rushed on to my little home, only to find the banks of the big ditch this side had burst, and water was rushing downhill to meet the coming tide from the Platte. I could go no further but could see that the boys from the corral were loading my things into the wagon. They had to swim the horses before they got through, and here *we* were in a bad plight ourselves. We were kindly taken in by a friend whose home was high and dry, and remained several days. The vacant rooms at the barracks were thrown open to the homeless, and here we are again in our old quarters where little "Bert" was born. Where we used to walk over to the east side on dry sand or elevated foot bridge, or wagon bridge, now runs a mighty torrent, spanned by a rope extension bridge. A ferry has been built across the Platte, and scenes of disorder and destruction are everywhere. People are groping in the slime and mud of the receding waters for their things, as most of the houses were left standing in the inundated district.

I have not had any of my queer impressions for a long time, until the other night, after I had gone to bed, I seemed to feel there was going to be a fire! I could not sleep, and could not impress By at all. He snored away while I laid in fear and trembling. I actually got up and put my valuables and a little money we had under my pillow, fixing my clothes ready to jump into, even placing my shoes and stockings on a chair in easy reach, then crept back to bed, feeling foolish enough, and had just gotten into a sleep, when the cry of "Fire! Fire!" startled us, and all was hurry and confusion, I exclaiming, "I knew it all the time!" The large commissary building where a large amount of government stores are kept, burned to the ground, doing no further damage, so all we had to do was to go back and settle our scattered household goods again. It seems there is one excitement after another, until I wonder I'm not white-headed. We are hearing of Indian depredations and scouting parties are out now from the barracks. Co. "H" is now and has been for some months stationed at Fremonts Orchard to guard the settlers. Bro. Sam is a member of that company. We stopped overnight with them as we came from Neb. City. There had been a light engagement, and I am all the time looking for news of another, as the Indians are no longer peaceable.

We have had a few weeks of comparative quiet with only occasional rumors of Indian troubles. We had always felt secure here in Denver, but were aroused from that feeling by one night of horror. On the evening of the 19th By, with almost *all* of the men from the barracks, had gone up to Denver to a political meeting. I sat in our room with the surgeon's wife, reading aloud some thrilling story from the "N.Y. Ledger." Our babies were sweetly sleeping and all was quiet and serene. It was about 11 o'clock that a horseman, one of our soldiers, came tearing up the road, dismounting before our door. He knocked furiously. I opened it, expecting something had happened, but what was my horror to hear him gasp out, as his knees knocked together, and his eyes almost starting from their sockets, "Run, wimmen! Run for your lives, the Injuns are coming three thousand strong! Run for the brick building at Denver! Governor's orders! But don't get skeered." (I was already about paralyzed.) "Mrs. Sanford, you tell the folks down the row while I go around," and away he went to the outside quarters. Mrs. Towles immediately went into hysterics, while I started to give the alarm, but when the woman came to the first door I went to, I could not utter a word My tongue had cleaved to the roof of my mouth. By this time I could hear the shrieks of women and children as the flying messenger went his rounds. By an effort of will power, I overcame my terror, and was soon back to my room, where my friend was wringing her hands in agony. We could hear bells ringing and the distant sound of confusion. In a very few moments the barracks were empty, the people on the road to Denver. I knew that By would come to me, and if I started he could not find me. Beside, I could not leave my friend with her two babies nor could I run with mine, so we concluded to stay where we were for a while, thinking it as safe there as on the road to town alone. Very soon By came. He did not seem so excited, as he hardly believed it, but he said we had better go, as there was not a living soul left at the barracks, as probably if there was an attack they would come here first to seize ammunition and arms. We picked up a few little things for the children, and putting the babies in their buggy, started, walking quietly along, and by this time I had gotten over my fright and did not credit the rumor much. It was so dark we could hardly see an object. We had nearly reached the town when we heard a quick volley of shots, then shouts, and then a mighty rush of horsemen toward us. I dropped on my knees, expecting my time had come at last, when just ahead of us passed a band of loose mules that had stampeded. We came on then to the brick buildings, only to find them crowded to suffocation. Fearing a collapse of the building, we went with a friend into her cottage nearby. By was put on patrol duty, his beat being directly in front of the house. Time went by, and no Indians came.

Scouts had been sent out in every direction, alarming settlers as they went, and by daylight the streets were filled with families who had fled from their homes. The returning scouts had found no traces of the Indians, and finally this and the returning daylight gave us the feeling of security, and the "scare" was over, and in due course of time people returned to their homes. It all came from some old people living out a few miles, imagining some Mexican cattle drivers to be Indians, and in their fright running two miles to the stage station, where the alarm was sent to the Governor. It only developed the fact that had there been an attack such confusion and panic ensued that the Indians could have wiped out the town.

September, 1863 [*1864*]

We spent the summer at the barracks. Have moved to Denver again. Regular Arabs are we, changing so often our habitations. By has bought a "ranch," has given up his position as Forage Master for the government, and early in the spring we move to the ranch to become farmers, I suppose for life.

Indian troubles have increased, and fears are now entertained that Denver may really be attacked, and pickets are stationed in the outskirts constantly. We are prospering nicely, have plenty of room and some real nice furniture, but O! dear, to be back on Gold Hill in the little black cabin, where we had no fear of foes. By is hauling wood from his ranch, selling, and carries back the material for a house, as there is only a small log cabin there now. He has bought the hewn logs of the first printing office in Denver, the "Rocky Mountain News," so we can preserve some relic of the illustrious. But I'm not thinking of that. I feel there is a great risk in his going over a lonely road 10 miles, for bands of Indians have been seen, and murders have been committed as near as that to Denver. For weeks I have hardly slept without my clothes on, ready to flee at a moment's warning. Mr. Woods, one of the soldiers at the hospital nearby, is to come to my rescue should the Indians come. A man and wife are in the front rooms, but he is such a coward that I often wish he were away.

Woods came to the door last night about midnight, saying, "O! Mrs. Sanford, don't get scart, but you had better sleep with one eye open. I'll be on hand." Suffice to say I slept with both optics open to their fullest capacity, but nothing came of the rumor that there might be an attack. By is gone from 3 to 5 days a trip, and I never have a moment's peace after I say good-by until I see him again. There were some prisoners ransomed by Col. Wyncop from the Indians, Laura Roper and two children. They were taken captive last summer by the Indians not very far from the old home in Neb. I had them at my house for a while. The tales of their captivity were harrowing. Miss Roper was subjected to all the indignities usually given white captives, and the children were brutally treated by the squaws. The mother of little Bell was taken away by some distant band, and the poor little things left. She saw her father butchered, and only three years old, can and does recount the whole tragedy. I took her, thinking I might adopt her, but I could not stand it. She would wake from a sound sleep, and sit up in bed with staring eyes, and go in detail over the whole thing. She was scarred all over with the prints of arrow points that the squaws tortured her with. Dr. Brondsall has adopted her, where she will have medical care and good care otherwise.*

* On August 7, 1864, a war party of Cheyenne and Arapaho attacked the Eubank ranch on the Little Blue River near the "narrows" of the Oregon Trail. The site is near the present town of Oak in Nuckolls County, Nebraska. Laura Roper, Mrs. William Eubank, Jr., and two children, Isabelle Eubank and an infant boy, were captured and four persons killed. Miss Roper, Isabelle Eubank, and another captive child, Danny Marble, were turned over to Major Wynkoop from Fort Lyon on September 11, 1864. Accounts of the affair state that little "Belle" Eubank was never returned to her mother, who was released from the Indians in May, 1865.

CHAPTER TEN

The Ranch and Denver

March 15, 1865–January 15, 1866

March 15, [1865]

We are living on our ranch, our own home, a lovely tract of 160 acres 10 miles from Denver, about 10 from the foot of the mountains. I feel content. By is preparing to farm a few acres. Mr. John McBroom furnishes seed and By does the farming on the shares. We have chickens and are making a garden. By has a shop and does repairing for the neighbors, and things for once look prosperous. Our house is very comfortable and looks more homelike than any place we have ever had, and *is Our Own*. I help By all I can and little "Bert" is happy all the day long.

April 15th [?]

There comes to us sad news, the assassination of President Lincoln. He died a martyr, died by the hand of a cowardly assassin, J. Wilkes Booth. He has been one of the noblest and best of our Presidents. How can our country spare him? O! what a cruel thing! The whole nation mourns. O could he have but lived to see Peace again in our land.

July [?] 4th

Denver again. What is life? We surely do not know what a day may bring forth! We thought ourselves settled for years on the ranch, and today finds us living in Denver. Our crops were just coming up so that the fields looked green in the slanting sunset, when the grasshoppers came, and in a few short hours destroyed the work of weeks, and about all the hopes we had. Of course others have suffered, but this has just about used us up. By was terribly discouraged, but as usual something "turned up." Through the influence and interest of an old friend of my Father's, who heard of our misfortune, By received an appointment as day watchman in the *U.S. Mint* in Denver, at a salary of $4 per day. It seems a kind Providence has followed us, and when an extremity comes there is a way out of it. We have a house nearby. A family have taken the ranch. O! well! I trust all is for the best. We could not stay there and starve, and it was too late to plant again, but I loved my country home.

October

By has a sister Emma who has come to make her home with us. Their parents are dead and she had no home but with strangers. She came thro Nebraska City where Dora is now living and where Father and Mother have bought a home. The old Hazel Dell has passed into the hands of strangers. They have had some hard times since we left, and I trust will enjoy their new home.

January 15, 1865 [1866]

The year of '65 ['66] dawns upon us fair and beautiful. It finds us residents of another home in the extreme suburbs of southern Denver. My brother Will is with us, By's brother George also, and we are quite a large family. Times are hard, Indian troubles causing high prices by their cutting off trains with supplies, as all we get comes over those plains in wagons. George was in a fight, but came out unharmed.

And now my "little book" I am about to the end. But before its close I bring to your notice my baby girl. On the 22nd of December she came, a dimpled, blue-eyed, brown-haired darling. We call her "Dora Bell," and altho hard times are with us, and troubles surround us, we are happy. Life now has much in store for us.

With my two little ones, I will have less time to journalize. I hope to spend it in caring for them in helpless infancy, training their young minds through childhood, on up through life, should they be spared to me. I pray for grace, patience, and judgement, and for long and useful lives for us all. I shall keep this book as a reminder of the past, and a help for the future.

MOLLIE

EPILOGUE

MOLLIE AND BY were to live long and useful lives as citizens of Denver. By was soon promoted from his post as watch man to the melting and refining department and remained employed at the United States Mint for forty years. He was a member of the commission which selected the site for the State University at Boulder and served as a trustee of the University. He died in Denver on November 27, 1914, at the age of eighty-eight. Mollie's death occurred less than three months later, on February 6, 1915. She was seventy-six. Throughout their lives Mollie and By remained attractive people, and Mollie is remembered as a "tower of strength" and the "balance wheel" of the family.

Hazel Dell, the Nebraska farm, was sold by Mollie's parents in 1865, and they moved to Nebraska City, where the father followed his trade as a carpenter. He helped build the Otoe County courthouse and, after moving to Lincoln in 1878, became a superintendent of construction on the new state capitol building. Mrs. Dorsey died in 1880 and Mr. Dorsey in 1888. After his wife's death, he had made his home with his youngest daughter, Ada, in Fullerton, Nebraska.

Mollie's brothers William, Charles, and George Denton were dead at the time of their father's death. George had been a carpenter and contractor and had lived in Lincoln and worked on the Nebraska state capitol building with his father. The annotator has not been able to determine what happened to Samuel.

Mollie's sisters all married. Dora's husband, Samuel Harris, served during the Civil War in the Fortieth Iowa Volunteers. After the war they lived a year in Iowa and then moved to Nebraska City, where he was a carpenter. In 1890 they were back in Denver and there they remained. Dora and eight of their nine children survived her husband, who died in 1919 at the age of eighty-seven.

Anna married Henry Harvey, a printer and newspaper publisher. The Harveys moved from Nebraska City to St. Louis in 1874. Mr. Harvey died in Denver in 1884.

Ada became the wife of Bradner Slaughter in 1866. He engaged in the manufacture of soap at Nebraska City and Omaha, after which, in 1879, he was a banker at Fullerton, Nebraska, and for a time United States Marshal for Nebraska. He was then appointed as a paymaster of the United States Army and served in this capacity until his death in Omaha in 1909. Ada and their six children survived him.

Mollie and By's son, Albert Byron Sanford, who was born at Camp Weld September 22, 1862, studied mining engineering at the University of Denver. After farming for a time, he opened an assay office in Denver and for twenty years was an assayer and mine examiner. In later years he served as curator of history for the State Historical Society of Colorado. He married Olive Snyder in 1890, and they were the parents of five children.

Dora Belle Sanford, Mollie and By's daughter, married Arthur Henry Williams, a major in the Colorado National Guard. It was to their son Albert Nathaniel Williams that Mollie willed her journal.

A NOTE ON THE EDITING OF MOLLIE'S JOURNAL

In 1895, Mollie Dorsey Sanford made a holograph copy of her journal, and destroyed the original (see opposite page 1). Some of her poems have been omitted, a few errors in spelling have been corrected, and the punctuation has been edited for clarity, but in all other respects the text of this book is an exact transcript of the 1895 holograph copy. There are some obvious errors in dating, but Mollie's dates are retained in every case. Corrections are added in brackets following her original entries.

ACKNOWLEDGMENTS

The University of Nebraska Press wishes to express its thanks to Mr. Albert N. Williams, Sr., for granting permission to publish his grandmother's journal, for his loan of the holograph copy, and for furnishing helpful information concerning the lives of his grandparents. We are indebted to Mr. R. E. Dale of the Nebraska State Historical Society for much of the information used in the footnotes concerning Mollie's acquaintances in Nebraska City; and to the State Historical Society of Colorado for biographical material concerning Byron N. Sanford. The Press is grateful to Mrs. Phyllis Winkelman, Director of Education, Nebraska State Historical Society, who first called the journal to its attention.